Eric Mitchell
Executive Vice President
www.GoldStarMtg.net
(310) 356-7388 ext. 729

Street Smart Selling

How to Be a Sales Superstar

by

Daniel Milstein

Street Smart Selling

Copyright © 2014 by Daniel Milstein

ISBN: 978-0-9835527-7-2 (paperback)
ISBN: 978-0-9835527-8-9 (hardcover)
ISBN: 978-0-9835527-9-6 (eBook)

Illustrations by Martin Bucella

Visit our website at
www.DanMilstein.com
for more information.

Gold Star
PUBLISHING
A DIVISION OF GOLD STAR MORTGAGE FINANCIAL GROUP

This book is dedicated to my exceptionally hardworking co-workers at Gold Star Mortgage Financial Group. I appreciate your professionalism, integrity, and commitment to help build Gold Star into a world-class, family-oriented company.

Contents

A Foreword by Mike Posner

Singer, Billboard Top 10 songwriter, and producer

There are many sales books available for those wanting to increase their production.

This one is different.

It is written by a salesman who became an executive who still considers himself a salesman.

Of course, you want to know that its author, Dan Milstein, is a success, an expert in his field who has something compelling to offer – something that you want to read.

But I don't need to focus on that here. The basic fact is that through hard work Dan became the top-producing mortgage originator in the country, and eventually the founder of Gold Star Financial, which now finances over $1 billion in loans annually and was named one of *Inc.* Magazine's 500 fastest growing companies.

One of the important lessons I've learned from Dan is the principal of "ABC" (Always Be Closing).

Many salespeople turn off their sales radar at the end of the work day.

Not Dan – he never stops selling. After reading this book, neither will you.

I've had an opportunity to observe Dan in a wide variety of situations; at hockey games, concerts, and even during the Sochi Winter Olympic Games. He lives and breathes sales. And that approach makes him the ideal author for this book.

The sales strategies Dan writes about in this book work. I've seen firsthand how he has used them in practice and how he has taught others to do the same. Dan's formula for success is a combination of passion, commitment to excellence, an amazing work ethic, and a series of proven strategies that he outlines in the following pages.

If you're an average salesperson who wants to become more successful, Dan's book will provide the roadmap you've been seeking. If you are already a top producer in your field, you'll find new insights to help you continue to thrive in a competitive field.

I join Dan in wishing you much success.

- Mike Posner
Relate, Love, Inspire

Preface

It is hard to believe that, if circumstances had been a little bit different, I actually might have been something other than a salesman. I have spent most of my professional life in sales, and at this point I can't imagine having a different career.

Growing up in Ukraine, we faced far greater challenges than trying to decide on a career. Even if my young friends and I had been inclined to wonder about future employment opportunities, a career in sales would probably not have been on my list. There were no real salespeople in Ukraine, since there was nothing much to sell. During the Socialist period in the Soviet Union there was always a lack of merchandise in stores, which were basically run by state-appointed directors who monopolized supply and demand. Unlike other countries where you could buy almost anything, if you wanted a television set or kitchen table, you'd place an order and then be told how long the wait would be.

A lack of opportunity was one of the reasons my parents made the courageous decision to leave our homeland in search of a new life in America. We arrived in 1991, full of hope and fiercely determined to meet the challenges before us. I couldn't imagine then how profoundly this move would impact me and certainly my future career.

Being hired at my local McDonald's restaurant as a high school junior was my first important work opportunity. My initial job was to clean the floors and bathrooms. While some people might be discouraged by this menial assignment, I saw this as the first step to achieving the American Dream. When I subsequently worked extremely hard to win a place in McDonald's Management Training Program, I knew that greater opportunities were within my grasp.

Although early on I was developing key habits that would yield great dividends in sales, my first realization that I was a "born salesman" came much later, after working in the lending industry for a few years. After a couple of failures as a mortgage broker, I began the trial and error process of fine-tuning my overall approach to work. Failure is a great teacher and certainly helped me to get on the right track.

I knew I wanted to be exceptionally successful, but wasn't sure how to measure my goal. Then, in

1999, I was on an airplane and opened the April issue of Mortgage Originator Magazine, which featured the annual Top Originator List. From that moment on, I had my first true measuring stick of success. I was determined to be on that list, and it inspired me to work even harder.

Because of my fascination with sales, it didn't really seem like work. I was intrigued with every aspect of selling and consumed with learning everything I could to perfect what I considered my lifelong profession. I loved having a detailed command of product knowledge, overcoming objections and the excitement at making the sale. It's been almost two decades since I closed my first loan, yet I still have a great feeling every time I am able to help a customer achieve their goal. I have never lost my passion.

One year after making it my mission to be on the Top Originators List, I found myself ranked in the top 20 out of 550,000 loan originators from throughout the country. I felt a deep satisfaction knowing I had overcome my earlier challenges—everything from learning the English language to gaining a better grasp of the mortgage lending profession. While I have never really focused on personal awards, that first major acknowledgement motivated me to strive for even greater results.

Since the publication of my first book, *The ABC of Sales*, which has been a best seller and won a number of prestigious awards, I have had an opportunity to talk with many salespeople at conferences, book signings and other events. I am frequently asked, "How do I become a top producer?" This is a topic I touched on in *The ABC of Sales* and one that I began to analyze in great detail. Through these conversations and my own experience and research, I began to formulate an answer about what it takes to become a sales superstar.

I have met many highly successful salespeople in various professions and have learned more about the steps they followed to earn their way to stand among the best. I have also known many other salespeople who, for whatever reason, haven't yet attained maximum success. You may be one of those individuals. While I know some salespeople lack the work ethic, motivation, or other critical attributes needed to reach the upper level, it is clear that many are simply not sure of the necessary strategies to help achieve their ambitious sales goals. They are stuck in first or second gear, unable to move further in the right direction.

I decided to write this book to share some of the techniques and ideas that helped me grow from someone who absolutely "sucked" as a salesman to someone who eventually achieved great success and became the CEO of a leading nationwide company.

Street Smart Selling is written for all salespeople who desire to excel at optimum levels, by a salesman who has weathered the same "ups and downs" that most of you are experiencing. Although my sales experience is in mortgage banking, the principles and strategies highlighted throughout the book can be applied to selling in almost any industry. I have tried to provide a framework you can tailor to your personal situation, along with the motivation to discover your own game plan and strategies. I have supplemented my own effective methods and personal experiences with the diverse insights from high-achieving sales professionals in other fields.

This book is also designed as a resource for sales managers who are responsible for helping to make their salespeople successful. I hope these managers will gain an even better understanding of how they can open new doors for their sales teams.

Even the most successful salespeople should never be totally satisfied. They know that it's dangerous to rest on past victories. They want to be assured they are continually doing everything possible to be the best in their profession. That is my heartfelt wish that you will become a sales superstar in your company, your market, and your industry. In doing so, you will become a superstar in life.

Chapter One
A Reality Check

Obstacles are necessary for success because in selling, as in all careers of importance, victory comes only after many struggles and countless defeats. - Og Mandino

I know just how you feel. It's near midnight and you're exhausted. You haven't been able to sleep because you have something serious on your mind: the monthly sales quota. You started your job full of inspiration and enthusiasm; the possibilities seemed endless. In fact, you've been doing moderately well until the recent slowdown. Or until too many competitors invaded your sales territory.

You think your job – or at least your anticipated commission – may be on the line. The sales manager is looking over your shoulder, waiting for your production to improve.

Or perhaps you're doing relatively well by an "average" salesperson's standards, but you aren't able to break through to become a true sales superstar.

Either way, your family and friends can sense your frustration; there is obviously something different about you. You are constantly on edge. Of course, you don't like the situation and want a remedy.

Fast.

We've all been there. I certainly have. Although I have always had the sales gene, when I started selling there were several rough patches. That's when I began doubting my own abilities.

About 20 years ago, I landed my first real career-oriented job at a large, well-known bank. What I lacked in skill, I made up for with enthusiasm and a passion for sales. I didn't have a clue as to what I was doing and it showed. My co-workers talked behind my back and my bosses watched my performance with microscopic attention.

Because I had arrived in this country just a few years earlier, I faced more of a challenge than most. I hadn't mastered the English language yet and my accent was still thick. I didn't have a mentor to guide me. Most of the customers who did understand my speech didn't take me seriously because I was so young. I looked and sounded like a teenager. I knew that if I was going to keep my first real "grown up" job, I'd have to figure it out on my own.

And so I did.

I read a variety of sales books, carefully watched my colleagues in action, and developed a list of what I considered to be the best strategies available. About 30 days after beginning this new approach, I had begun to turn things around. Customers were no longer rejecting my presentation – I was getting sales. In another few months, I was surpassing my own expectations and making more sales than anyone else on my team. I had developed a seemingly fool-proof plan that helped turned everything around.

In this book, I'm going to share my formula for success for the first time. I believe it will help all salespeople—whether you're selling mortgages, computers, insurance policies or cars—get to the next level in their career.

Some of the things I will discuss are:

• How to change your mental attitude so that it is an aid, not a hindrance.

• Proven tools and strategies to get you on the fast-track to success.

• Finding what motivates you and discovering how that motivation can help you achieve professional and personal goals.

• Identifying your strengths and how to use them to your advantage.

The sales techniques covered in this book will

work for you, whether you are a relatively new salesperson looking for an edge, a frustrated salesperson who seeks to overcome a few challenges, or a moderately successful individual who wants to be a superstar. I know they will work because they are the same essential steps that helped me move beyond a few difficult sales slumps. They are the same techniques that we've shared with our employees throughout the country, techniques that helped us achieve a special milestone: being recognized three times on the *Inc.* 500 list of fastest-growing companies. Reading this book may save you a few thousand dollars in sales seminars.

While becoming a sales superstar isn't an overnight process, you can be on your way to a greater level of success within 30 to 90 days, if you want it badly enough.

So the question is, do you?

Chapter Two
Developing a Superstar Mindset:
Adjusting Your Attitude

You cannot tailor-make the situations in life but you can tailor-make the attitudes to fit those situations.
- Zig Ziglar

Now is the time to make sure you have the right mindset to help you achieve sales greatness.

You may be full of doubt. Maybe you have already tried a menu of different techniques that haven't resulted in a significant improvement in your sales performance. You have read books, listened to motivational tapes and attended seminars, but you still haven't been able to achieve the desired results.

You may have to change your attitude.

"But I do have a good attitude," you may say to yourself. Really? I have noticed a major difference between salespeople who perform at a high level and those who don't. The ones who "kill it" – and end up advancing faster and higher than others – have a very specific attitude and mindset. They don't see problems, they only see challenges. Furthermore, they look forward to those challenges with fierce enthusiasm that other people don't demonstrate. They continually push themselves.

Perception is Key

You may think you have the right attitude. But what do your co-workers, clients, prospects, and management think about it?

If you come across as negative for any extended period of time, it will weigh you down and impact your sales efforts.

You may think you have a right to feel and behave the way you do, as someone who has had a difficult time succeeding. After all, you are frustrated that your hard work hasn't paid off as planned. But in case you forgot a basic lesson, your customers don't care. All they care about is that you are able to give them what they want. They don't want to hear about how hard your life is and how tired you are or how bad things are at home. They don't want to know that:

• Your sales quota is too high.

• You think the competition has better products.

- Your company doesn't provide enough support.
- Or any other excuse.

Your prospects only want to know how your product or service will help them, and that you have their best interests at heart, not your own.

An Attitude Adjustment

It would be nice if we could wave a magic wand to make everything better. But that's not possible, so instead the key is to change your mindset and attitude.

Take a deep breath. It isn't as serious as you think. Your challenges aren't as significant, your roadblocks to success not as big as they seem. It may help to take a day off, or focus on something non work-related to help shed some of the negative feelings. Some say taking a nap, watching a football game, or playing with your kids can be like rebooting a computer. Get your mind off the negative so you can come back, re-charged and with a new attitude.

Everyone goes through rough patches. And I mean everybody. You've probably heard the story of how Babe Ruth hit the most home runs of all time, but also had 1,330 strikeouts. Success is defined not only by what you accomplish, but how many times you get back up after you've been knocked down. I've been knocked down a number of times. Getting up again isn't always easy, but I've learned that we define our own success. We can't let anyone else do it for us.

Have your pity party and then get over it. Some-times it feels good to feel sorry for ourselves and to encourage everyone to commiserate with us. But that doesn't do much to help boost your short or long-term sales. So if you must feel sorry for yourself, make it brief and then move on.

Success breeds more success. Celebrate every suc-cess you make. It may help to make a list of your successes. At Gold Star, we encourage salespeople and others to recognize their small accomplishments – such as making a few new contacts and starting a new marketing strategy – as well as the more substantial production achievements. Make a list of every success and you'll be reminded that success is a habit.

I read a great list of the "20 Things the Rich Do Every Day" by Tom Corley. In this case I prefer to call it the "Things Successful People Do Every Day." Included in his list are the following:

- "67% of wealthy write down their goals vs. 17% of poor."
- "81% of wealthy maintain a to-do list vs. 19% of poor."
- "88% of wealthy read 30 minutes or more each day for education or career reasons vs. 2% of poor."
- "63% of wealthy listen to audio books during commute to work vs. 5% of poor."
- "79% of wealthy network five hours or more each month vs. 16% of poor."

Also, remember to enjoy the process. As someone reminded me several years ago, "Success is a journey, not a destination."

Don't Lose Your Passion for Sales

The salespeople with the best attitudes are those who never lose their passion for sales. Passion helps you get through the ups and downs of sales. You can "endure" a career without passion, but you cannot be a long-term success unless you love what you do.

From my first experience as a salesman, I have had the passion, the enthusiasm to sell, even though I have faced the same doubts and frustrations that most salespeople do. As with any other profession, passion means truly enjoying what you do and looking forward to the challenges rather than complaining about the obstacles. All salespeople deal with daily rejection; customers shaking their heads, abruptly closing doors, hanging up the phone, leaving without the sale. Having a genuine love for the sales process helps ensure you can thrive while dealing with the inevitable challenges, ranging from dismal economic conditions, product delivery complications, customer complaints, or basic everyday rejection.

You have a passion for sales if you:

• Wake up every morning looking forward to doing the job. Sure, there will be days when it's hard to get out of bed, but if you're truly passionate about what you do, then the up days will far outweigh the down days.

• Not only handle rejection from customers, vendors and others, but actually see every "no" as a valuable learning lesson. I'm a firm believer that the sale begins when the customer says "no." You can't take a negative reaction personally. Just like a positive response, it is a chance to learn and grow. Take what you learn from a rejection so that you can apply it to your next sales opportunity. Even today, though I've been selling for decades, I'm still learning and growing.

• Welcome the chance to talk about sales "after hours." A car salesman friend of mine told me he was even able to discuss his dealership's newest models as he sat in the dentist's chair. Now that is enthusiasm!

• Actually enjoy getting work-related calls at night or on weekends. I often share the story about the airline pilot who called our office late at night to leave a message about his interest in obtaining a mortgage. Gold Star has established a firm policy whereby our office phones are transferred to individual cell phones after hours. As a result, I received the call as a group of us relaxed in a restaurant. The pilot was surprised when I answered at two a.m. and took his loan application...on a cocktail napkin. He was impressed that someone was available to help when he really needed it, and has since referred numerous friends and family members to me. I still have the framed napkin on my office wall, which is a great reminder that customers value accessibility.

• Are as enthusiastic selling now as the day you made your first sale. You want to maintain the excitement, the fresh attitude that salespeople have when they first start out. Focus, clear your mind, and avoid thinking about other non-essentials. You should avoid entering your office if you don't feel passion for sales, your products and services, and the customers you serve.

When I have the opportunity to speak to salespeople at conferences, on college campuses, and other occasions, I give them part or all of my "graduation" speech. This is when I have the chance to share some of my personal experiences and, ideally, provide additional motivation to encourage them to be the best they can be. The talks vary, but always have a similar theme—"Passion and drive and a lot more will make you successful."

I explain that many skills can be taught, that we can learn the basics of our various professions and the "nuts and bolts" of sales techniques. "It's nearly impossible to teach someone to have the passion for sales and the drive to excel at the highest level," I explain. "But you will need both. So do a self-analysis today to see if you have them and make the appropriate adjustments as soon as possible. Don't be afraid to experiment, to make things happen. Most importantly be willing to make mistakes; this is how good salespeople become better."

A positive, passionate attitude won't necessarily make you a sales superstar, but I guarantee you'll never be a true success without it.

Chapter Three
Success Requires Hard Work:
You Can't Stumble Into Greatness

Be not afraid of greatness: some are born great, some achieve greatness, and some have greatness thrust upon them.
- William Shakespeare

Look around – they are everywhere. You see them in every profession, and sales is no different. They are mediocre, average performers.

All my sales associates know that for me, "average" just doesn't cut it in business. Average means you are virtually indistinguishable from your competitors, so clients and prospects will have little reason to remember you.

While I am impressed with the vast number of disciplined, hardworking salespeople in various professions, I am always amazed by those who think achieving these high levels of success will be easy. They want the benefits of being a sales superstar without putting in the extra effort. They don't seem to understand that the "no risk, no reward" idea is an inescapable fact of life in sales. Top performers have learned that you can't stumble into greatness. It takes preparation, patience, and especially hard work!

I have long been intrigued about the characteristics of top-producing salespeople. Based on conversations with numerous professionals in various fields, I am convinced that, while some of them find a direct path to achieving great success, most follow a more circuitous route. I know firsthand that no matter how dedicated you are, there will always be speed bumps that will delay your quest to be a sales superstar. As

I recounted in my first book, *The ABC of Sales*, I initially failed as a mortgage broker because I lacked the necessary sales skills and background to close a loan. However, that unfortunate experience taught me valuable lessons and gave me further incentive to eventually become a top producer.

Your Motivation

It is important that salespeople assess their motivation for desiring to be a top producer. There are certainly different reasons for wanting to become one of your industry's best:

Achieving financial goals – Obviously, as your sales increase, so do your commissions, which can move you closer to personal goals like securing the well-being of your family, or enjoying early retirement. However, as I caution our salespeople and those I meet elsewhere, do not let this be your only driving force.

Obtaining other perks – The more sales success you achieve, the more likely it is that you will receive other rewards, including marketing support and incentive trips. However, it is easy to begin accepting the "extras" as your right, rather than a bonus. It is better to view perks as you would nice weather: something to be appreciated and enjoyed, but not always under your complete control and never guaranteed.

Ego gratification –There are salespeople who want to become superstars primarily for peer recognition and the "bragging rights." As you continue along the route to becoming a superstar, it is essential to maintain the proper perspective. While I have been acknowledged as a top producer, I don't dwell on this achievement. I always remember the simple phrases an experienced salesman stressed to me: "You are only as good as your next deal," "Don't rest on your past glory," and "As soon as you believe you 'have arrived' (are a success), it's time to retire." Those statements may sound a little extreme, but it isn't wise to fall into the trap of believing how great you are. The real superstar graciously accepts this top-producer reputation without letting it become a distraction.

Know What Motivates You

Be sure you know why you want to become a sales superstar. You have to understand what pushes you, whether it is financial compensation, ego gratification, company recognition or something else. List your top two reasons now and then look at them again after three months. What's changed?

You may need to dig a little deeper to find your true motivation. It needs to be something beyond the glitz and glamour that any type of superficial success provides. Initially, my principal motivation was to make my mother proud and to prove to others I was successful. While my mother preferred that I become a doctor, I discovered that my goal was simply to have a well-respected white-collar job. I knew that being a success would prove to everyone that I had chosen a worthy profession. Maybe your motivation is to make your children proud or to prove all the doubters wrong. In addition to any monetary rewards, find something within you that will keep you going when things look dark.

The Superstar Yardstick

How do you measure superstar success? Is it based solely on your annual sales? Ultimately you define your own success. You are the one to determine what success means. Performance in many professions – like teaching, law enforcement, and engineering – is judged on a combination of subjective and objective criteria that may also include industry association involvement and community service. However, unlike teachers or other professionals, salespeople are primarily evaluated by how many units they sell, such as their monthly or annual sales total of mortgage loans, insurance policies, autos, houses, computers, or clothing. That doesn't discount the importance of other more subjective variables such as community involvement and professional reputation; it's just that our overriding goal is to sell, and selling is the focus of this book.

In the mortgage-lending profession, the main barometer of being a top producer is the number of loans and total dollar volume closed annually, as indicated by "Top Originator" lists that several industry publications have created. Some experts cite 250 loans and $35 million of personally closed loans in a year to be the baseline for loan originators ranked as top producers, although this varies depending on market conditions. I have been ranked as the lending industry's number one originator for several years, and have helped thousands of clients obtain their home financing. The insurance, real estate, and other industries have their own measure of ultimate success.

Not having a formal, definable superstar benchmark in your profession shouldn't preclude you from establishing a specific goal. If no such standards currently exist, create your own. Compare notes with other successful salespeople in your market and determine what might be an appropriate target for which to aim. You don't have to focus solely on raw numbers. I know a computer salesman who set a goal of selling an office computer software program every week. But in order for the sale to "count," he wanted his customers to be in a profession that involved talking to other people. The salesman wanted to be sure that there was always an opportunity for his new customers to help "spread the word" about his products and generate referrals. So he selected professionals such as dentists, barbers, nail stylists and teachers. His simple strategy worked. In his first week of doing this, he had several people call him to ask how the software program could help their business.

Be sure to consider whether you want to be a superstar within your own company, your local market, or the industry. At each level, you will find steeper mountains to climb.

Build Your Yardstick

If no formal measurement for sales success exists for your industry, create your own. Start by listing the top five salespeople at your company. Then try to rank the top 10 producers in your market (based on information from other salespeople and local business groups). This will give you a place to start, to measure yourself against others in your field.

Strive for #1

Based on my own background and "Always Be Closing" (ABC) philosophy, I tend to emphasize a "Be Number One" attitude, which is an integral part of the Gold Star culture. I believe that if you are going to do a good job in sales or anything else, you should always seek to be the best, thereby having a better chance of reaching the top. If you don't reach your ultimate goal by the end of one, two, or five years, keep working at it. You will still be performing at a higher level than ever before.

I also stress that salespeople should initially be

concerned about their own production, rather than trying to outdo more seasoned professionals. I recall one fledging salesman who worked 16 hours a day for three weeks, and while he turned in a solid quarterly performance, he was disappointed not to be ranked with the company's top salespeople. I asked him to stop by my office to discuss his goals and he immediately began talking about outperforming the other salespeople in the next quarter. I explained that he needed to focus on achieving his own goals—improving each week, month and quarter—instead of beating himself up or trying to out-sell his peers. By trying to constantly surpass your personal bests, you have a better chance of attaining top producer results.

Once you know your motivation for becoming a top salesperson and have your own yardstick by which to measure your success, you are nearly ready to continue the journey. Before taking another step, you must be absolutely certain you have the passion and drive to achieve ambitious goals.

Do you?

Chapter Four
Planning Ahead:
Don't Leave Home Without Your Compass
By failing to prepare, you are preparing to fail.
- Benjamin Franklin

I know you wouldn't drive cross country without a map. How can you become a sales superstar without a detailed plan? To become a top tier salesperson, you may have to refine your planning methods.

Can you become a top-producing salesperson without a formal, written plan? I know a number of great salespeople who most likely never wrote such a document. However, a written plan ensures that you will have a better chance of succeeding at a high level for a longer period. It enables you to work smarter, taking a proactive approach rather than reacting to challenges along the way.

If you believe as I do that failure is not an option, then you will view a plan as a roadmap that will guide you safely to sales success. If you do not have a written plan yet, start developing one today. If you do have one, this is an ideal time to review and see if you can make it even better.

Planning Essentials

In case you've forgotten the basics of developing a plan, here is a quick refresher course:

• *Goal* – You need a concrete goal, such as a dollar amount. The more specific you are, the more likely you are to achieve it. You need to further break down your major goal into the steps required to accomplish it. How many prospects would you need to see on an annual, monthly and weekly basis? How many specific products or services would you need to sell? You also must establish time limits to ensure progress.

• *Situation* – What is your current market like? Describe the big picture, which includes current economic conditions, as well as your local focus that might involve the competition, special challenges, and notable opportunities. This helps ensure that the plan is relevant to your immediate circumstances.

• *Audiences* – Develop a clear vision of your primary sales targets or niches. Perhaps your product or service appeals to a broad group, the "anyone who needs and is able to afford it" category. On the other hand, you may be able to break your customer base into segments, such as first-time buyers, seniors, Gen X prospects, teachers, medical professionals and others. This will also give you a good idea of how you might define your business base. You must know enough about your sales targets so that you can appeal to them in just the right ways.

• *Strategies* – How will you accomplish your goals? What action steps, including marketing tactics and operational procedures, will you employ? Start with what has been most effective in the past and add new elements based on marketplace changes, budgets and other factors. Make sure you include daily as well as the more long-term strategies. Your daily plan is more than the customary "to do" list of call-backs, appointments scheduled and other necessary actions. It should prompt you to take incremental steps that will move you closer to fulfilling a major goal, such as initiating a social media campaign or establishing a referral system.

The End to the Beginning

Start with your ultimate goal and work backwards. If your main desire is to earn $200,000 a year, figure how many sales at your current commission rate you will need to close. How many prospects will you need to meet in order to close that volume? How many calls per day will you need to make in order to arrange the necessary meetings with your prospects? This basic guide will give you a quick look at what you need to accomplish so you can reach your primary goal.

• *Resources* – What do you need to accomplish the plan? Evaluate what you have at your disposal. In addition to cash resources, you need to consider time, access to knowledge, and the ability to work with special talents at your company or elsewhere. You may need to hire an assistant, invest in your marketing budget, or update your technology.

• *Monitoring* – You must include a system to review your progress, measuring the results and determining what additional actions are necessary to achieve your goals. You have to evaluate them on a daily, weekly and monthly basis. Are you making more effort this week than you were last week? Are your co-workers doing better than you? If so, why? You must know how you're progressing to see where you need improvement and if you should continue on your current path or shift gears.

Like most salespeople, you will probably experience a series of gradual changes in the planning process. You should start with an informal plan that charts your preliminary direction to reach your first sales successes, which will then evolve into a more comprehensive process. When I began as a salesperson, my main goal was to talk with as many prospective customers as possible every day, believing that this would lead to sales and eventually a referral network that I could continue to build. In addition to sending various mailers, a primary strategy was to "wait for the phone to ring." However, I also began meeting with referral sources and advertising in the local newspaper. Although I lacked formal training in creating a master plan, this helped give me enough "real world" experience that I was able to fine-tune my approach.

I will admit that as a new salesman, my first plans were sketchy, a few handwritten pages at best. Then one day I made a career-changing discovery. I had finally organized my file of notes into a well-researched formal business plan. As part of the planning process, I realized that certain marketing strategies had a much higher return on investment than others. I had an opportunity to make some fundamental changes and significantly increase my overall profitability. I soon developed specific six month, one-year, and five-year plans that have since proven to be key tools for increasing my sales volume.

A More Meaningful List

Divide your daily "to do" list into two parts: the basic tasks that need completion, such as returning calls, arranging meetings, completing sales and so on; and the results-oriented daily accomplishments. The latter are incremental steps that are directly tied to you reaching a specific goal, helping ensure that you make steady progress to accomplish your major goals and objectives.

Planning Tips

Here are a few additional planning tips:

• Don't wait until January to prepare your plan for the new year. The planning process should begin toward the end of the previous year. You can then make adjustments in early January.

• Develop a plan that is flexible enough to take advantage of changes in the marketplace.

• You shouldn't base your planning on what the

competition is doing, but it doesn't hurt to have an idea of their core marketing or other strategies. This information may give you ideas on new ways to modify your plan.

• Take advantage of available planning tools. For example, in addition to the numerous books and website resources, you can find some helpful project management applications for your smartphones and tablets. Search for other ideas that will help you become more efficient in the planning process.

Having a formal plan is a basic requirement for salespeople and other professionals. I am assuming you have one. You won't succeed without it.

Chapter Five
Implement the Plan: Use it or Lose it

Create a definite plan for carrying out your desire and begin at once, whether you are ready or not, to put this plan into action.

- Napoleon Hill

We all know the type: the salespeople who make big plans, but when it comes to action, they don't do anything. They are Dreamers, not Doers. If you want to be a sales superstar and start achieving even better results during the next three months, then you must be a Doer. You can create elaborate plans, but unless you take action, nothing is going to happen.

I have talked to a number of trainers and others who agree on a sad fact—too many salespeople develop a plan and then subsequently leave it untouched in a file folder. They may not even think about the plan again until a sales manager asks them how they intend to accomplish their goals. I know I have caught several of our salespeople off guard by asking "Let's take a look at your plan for the next six weeks."

"Plan your work and work your plan" is a well-known slogan used by training and business consultants. It may seem overly simplistic, yet the message is always timely and should be a constant reminder for all of us. You first need to develop an effective plan and then you must actually follow it. You have to "work it." This is an attitude we continually stress at Gold Star.

Some people may need a reminder that they need to use their plan. Of course, you can keep a copy of the plan on a pedestal in your office. If that seems too bold, add a "Plan Now" or "The Plan" sign to your desk. Or change your PC screen saver to: "Work that Plan."

Even more important than keeping the plan visible, you need to use it on a frequent basis. Do you compare your plan's directions with daily or weekly status updates? Do you adhere to the strategies you have outlined? Do you measure results on a regular basis? Do you make the appropriate adjustments?

Having a bound copy of the plan on your desk is pointless if you don't get past the Contents page.

Looking Forward

Top performers look beyond the basics. They realize that part of "using it" is keeping their plan fresh and relevant to changes that occur with their business. Salespeople are typically busy every day with their core responsibilities: selling, meeting new customers, explaining products or services, writing contracts, handling complaints, and many other tasks. It may not seem like there is much time to look ahead and consider future directions, yet that is exactly what you need to do. You must seek insights regarding issues like:

• **The General Economy** – Are current economic conditions expected to change significantly during the next six months to a year? How might that affect your local market?

• **Industry Trends** – Your particular profession may be undergoing a huge growth spurt, or it could be suffering from a slow period. Are major companies consolidating, and if so, will that give you greater or fewer opportunities?

• **Customer Demographics** – How your primary customer base is changing will be of particular interest. Do you envision a change in buying patterns? Are Generations X and Y expected to become a stronger component of your customer base?

Anticipate

Spend a few minutes each day evaluating how potential changes in the economy, your industry, and local market might impact your overall planning process and sales strategies. List them in two categories: those needing immediate attention and others that you could earmark for longer range action. If necessary, do additional research to confirm whether the factors will have a pronounced or minor influence. Keep track of the results.

Early in my sales career, I saw the need to look ahead at our local market conditions. For example, I realized that I could not continue to rely on Michigan's Big 3 automobile workers as a primary source of business, since the state's economy was slumping and massive layoffs were expected. I looked for ways to expand business beyond my backyard and began prospecting on a more regional basis. I continued this same focus as our company expanded, and this has extended to a national scale. In addition, while much of my first business came from our local immigrant population, I saw the need to explore other customer niches, such as professional athletes and law enforcement.

Take advantage of your industry's market surveys and other news of changing buying patterns. For example, if you know when people typically make major purchases of computer systems, houses, insurance policies or other products and services, you are in a better position to market to them accordingly. I recall first realizing that an increasing number of consumers would be using the Internet to seek sales information and make purchase decisions, so I began to do more Internet advertising. I did not possess any remarkable forecasting ability; I just saw the reports about people buying shoes, books, computers and many other items from their online stores.

It can also help to have a good understanding of your industry's current and future regulatory environment and how specific changes might impact sales. For instance, if you knew that a government or other agency was planning to restrict or otherwise modify the availability of a certain product category, you could plan ahead by converting to another product line.

Looking forward can force you to move beyond your comfort zone. If you are not familiar with market research techniques or other means of evaluating the future, start with the obvious. Conduct Internet research, read industry publications, attend conferences and discuss the issues with veteran salespeople and business experts.

Raising the Bar

Another essential part of the "use it (your plan)" concept is adjusting your annual sales goals. While a company sales manager may establish the basic target, you should also have the flexibility to adjust it upward to ensure even greater productivity. You don't want to be overly ambitious and possibly miss your number by a wide margin, but you should also avoid being too conservative and thereby lose the opportunity to grow. You won't be able to become one of the best unless you are willing to reach for higher goals.

If you aren't accustomed to increasing your sales projections, experiment by adjusting them upward by a comfortable margin for a six-month trial basis. If you reach that point too easily, then perhaps you want to raise it a bit higher. If attaining the higher goal is a struggle, you might lower it.

You must also be flexible. I have a great example of this. One of our salespeople told me he was going to reward himself with a trip to Miami if he closed $25 million in loans in one year. After five months, he had already reached $30 million, so I asked him when he was leaving for Miami. "I'm not," he told me. "Once I realized I was going to hit $25 million in half the time, I set my goal for $100 million for the year, and if I reach that, I'm going to Europe." I smiled and said that if he hit that goal, I would gladly pay for his airfare. The following January, I bought tickets to Paris for him and his wife.

Raise The Bar Comfortably

At the beginning of the year, set an ambitious but achievable sales goal based on the prior year's production and anticipated changes in your industry's growth. Review your sales volume on a quarterly basis to see how close you are to the projections. Try to raise the sales bar by a reasonable amount, such as 10 percent. You may wish to keep two sets of goals: the sales manager-approved quota and your own "raise the bar to superstar" figures.

It Is Your Responsibility

I understand you may be thinking, "I really don't have much control over my goals and sales strategies, so what's the purpose of developing and following a formal plan? Everything is dictated by my company. I just have to follow their guidelines."

That is a ridiculous notion. It's easy to rationalize a lack of extra effort by complaining that you don't have the opportunity to exceed company-imposed goals. Remember that in order to reach the highest level of success, you have to view yourself as a business, doing whatever it takes to reach your ultimate goals.

All salespeople have at least some control over how they approach their job, the planning process, and their ultimate success. It's easy to blame everyone else when things don't go your way. The economy is in a recession. Your co-worker didn't do what he was supposed to do. Don't worry about what anyone else is doing. You can only control yourself.

If you want to increase your sales volume, but believe that company restrictions don't provide much flexibility, use your imagination to determine the steps that you can take. For example, if you sell automobiles or modular homes for a company that requests you don't deviate from its standard marketing campaign, that probably does not preclude you from calling friends and relatives and asking them to refer their contacts to you. Make a few more cold calls, or email one more person. And nothing is stopping you from learning more about your industry, or brainstorming how you can continue to develop as a salesperson. Rather than focus on what is not possible, evaluate the areas over which you do have some control. And, if you think that the sales manager will not appreciate such an entrepreneurial approach, keep your plans to yourself.

If you're willing to do whatever is necessary, your sales will improve, perhaps even faster than you expected. But pay attention to your plan.

What Successful Salespeople Should Strive to Do Every Day

Start the morning with enthusiasm. As you already know, having a positive "can do" attitude makes a huge difference in how you follow through with the rest of your day.

Make effective use of drive time. Listen to an audio book, tape your "to do" list (safely) or just review your morning action plan.

Call a specific number of prospects. These can be brief calls to introduce yourself, obtain personal information to update your database and/or to see if you can answer questions.

Pay attention to your business plan. This can be as simple as reviewing various plan elements or adding a new idea.

Consider a new niche for your business. It might be one that you would like to develop either in the near future or on a long-term basis.

Call several past customers. Staying in touch with customers is vital. Call to ask how they and their families are doing, and if there is anything you can do to help.

Read local business publications. Spend a few minutes reviewing the "New Hires," "New Promotions," or "Local Milestones" section. Then send a "welcome" or "congratulations" card or email to those with whom you would like to do business.

Learn something new about your company, product and/or the competition. Each time you increase your knowledge base, you're potentially adding to your reputation as an expert.

Expand your strategic partner network. Add one or more of your newest referral sources or other VIP contacts.

Take time to really understand your clients' needs. Stop and reflect on your most recent conversations to make sure you continue to have their best interests in mind and that your contacts with them reflect that attitude.

Make a Sale. That is what we are here for. However, even if you don't close one sale, you can make significant progress toward this important goal. Each meeting, call, or email should move you that much closer.

Spend your time wisely. If possible, avoid long meetings and long breaks. Before taking off for a long lunch, think of the sales opportunities you might miss. Try to make each call to a client or prospect as productive as possible.

Show your appreciation. Acknowledge others – including a sales manager, assistant, or other associate – for their often unrecognized support. It doesn't take long and can further help establish a positive working relationship.

Return all calls and emails. Customers and prospects often complain about not getting timely responses to their questions or concerns. Before leaving each day, follow up with a quick email or brief call to emphasize that you are taking care of them.

Plan the next day. A good way to set the tone for the following day is to outline a few of your major goals. This isn't just the traditional "to do" list, but rather a highlight of a few core activities – possibly scheduled at morning, mid-day and afternoon – that you believe will have a big impact on your sales success.

Chapter Six

Distinguish Yourself from the Competition:
Stand Up and Out

The way to gain a good reputation is to endeavor to be what you desire to appear. - Socrates

"I'm not sure that he or she is any better than other salespeople. They are all about the same."

You never want anyone saying that about you.

Salespeople must stand out; they must differentiate themselves from others in their market. If your prospective customers don't know why you are better, you risk losing business to a competitor who does have a distinctive reputation.

It is absolutely critical to differentiate yourself from other salespeople in order to enjoy long-term success. I emphasize long-term because it is certainly possible to have temporary success as a competent, average salesperson without having that special identity. However, to become and remain a top producer for the long run, you have to stand out from the crowd.

People often continue to buy from a salesperson they know and like out of "habit" or loyalty. Customers who had a positive experience when they

made their initial purchase will often decide that it is convenient to keep buying from this same salesperson. However, if a more knowledgeable, experienced salesperson who provides amazing customer service approaches them later, they may very well decide it is time to make a change.

Assessing Your Difference

You may not have taken the time to analyze the ways customers will differentiate you from other salespeople. Chances are, you are so busy making calls and pursuing your goals that you may not have stopped to think what separates you from everyone else. For example, potential areas of differentiation are:

• **Product or Service Offering** – Does your product or service offer more features, something that makes your "commodity" different than the others? Before answering yes, keep in mind what may be most important to the consumer. They really want to know how those features will help them, and why your product is better than the competition.

• **Pricing** – Are your product/service fees about the same as theirs? Does a competitor offer a special "match your best price" or other program? Of course, you don't want your reputation to be all about low pricing. As I often say, "Great rates are irrelevant without great service."

• **Knowledge** – How does your understanding of and ability to communicate your products and programs compare to other salespeople? If you are able to impress customers with your expertise, they will know you can always provide them with the best options. Because of the Internet and the ready availability of other research tools, consumers have become more knowledgeable about the products and services in which they are interested. You must always convey the attitude that your expertise – the ability to help customers find solutions to their critical needs

– has great value. Just think of the story about the plumber who was able to unclog a homeowner's drain by lightly tapping the pipe. When the customer asked for an itemized bill to justify what he considered an excessive charge, the plumber wrote: "$80.50—fifty cents for the use of my special hammer and $80 for my expertise: knowing just where and how hard to hit the pipe."

Chart Your Difference

Create a list of the key features that might distinguish you from other salespeople. These include knowledge, service, product availability, convenience and anything else you consider important. You can also include such non-sales areas as your education, community involvement, and special honors. Include two columns: in one, list the features you feel are a strong part of your reputation as a salesperson, and in the other list what you believe customers think represent you. The goal is to make sure you and your customers have a similar view.

• **Niche Expertise** – You may have a reputation for being the expert in a specific area, such as "the expert in high end performance cars," "first time homeowner specialist" or "THE small business financial planner," but be cautious about defining yourself too narrowly. If your prospective customer base is exceptionally large, this might work to your advantage; however, you never want to exclude a substantial group of potential customers. While I have developed several effective niches, including the local immigrant population and professional athletes, Gold Star always emphasizes a more general customer base.

• **Customer Service** – People appreciate salespeople who go out of their way to understand their needs and help fulfill them. Those who "go the extra mile" with customer service generally get extra points over and above others who only provide the bare necessities. One of my sales associates actually traveled a long distance to a prison to meet with the incarcerated ex-husband of a customer, so the inmate could sign a quit-claim deed that was required for a new loan. I was also impressed when another of our salespeople helped a customer paint their house and make other minor repairs in order to meet underwriting stipulations. Perhaps you don't want to visit a prison or be a part-time painter. There are numerous other options. For example, do you make home deliveries and provide helpful educational materials? Are you available evenings and weekends? Do you send them helpful information about the product or service? Customers will always know when you are going out of your way to make their purchase a pleasant experience.

• **Your Sales Success** – The fact you are a top producer or number one in your market may be less important now than it was a decade ago when customers were overly impressed with their salesperson's production rankings.

• **Attitude** – While not as easy to promote, a positive attitude is also critical. I believe consumers appreciate talking with and buying from confident salespeople who are upbeat rather than negative.

You may not have control over all of these factors, such as pricing and product availability, but you need to be aware of how customers and others factor them in as part of your overall identity.

Ask Them

You also need a good objective understanding of how your customers and prospects actually view you. Survey a group of past customers and strategic partners, including those professionals you work with on a regular basis and others who provide referrals. Develop a brief written survey, or ask them during your regular phone conversations. Explain that you would like their frank opinion about how they see you as a sales professional. For example, ask them to rank you from 1-10 on your knowledge, service, product availability and personality. Even better, break down the vague "personality" component into more specific attributes, like patience, willingness to listen, overall demeanor and other attitude factors. You may find it takes considerable effort to obtain this type of information, but it can be helpful. We all know salespeople who are knowledgeable and experienced, but who are also overbearing or otherwise irritating.

In addition, you can encourage general comments about your overall image compared to other salespeople. For example, you might ask, "Why do you continue doing business with me rather than another salesman?" ("Because you have all the answers… go out of your way to help us… are always available when I call.")

You can also gain valuable feedback in a more informal way, during casual conversations with customers. Maybe you're asking them how their daughter's band recital went and in the conversation you happen to ask them what they're happy about with your service, and if appropriate, their opinion of your strengths and skills. I do this every chance I get – at business activities, social gatherings and even neighborhood parties where I encounter some of my customers. We'll be discussing current events or family news and if I see an opening in the conversation I will say something like, "I imagine you're all settled in your new home by now. I promised it would be a positive experience." I've received such responses as "We couldn't be happier…You made it seem so easy…You made us so comfortable by providing regular updates…We'll never go anywhere else for a mortgage…"

Having a better understanding of how your customers perceive you is important because their impressions are likely to differ in at least some areas from your own self-analysis.

It is also important to know how you are perceived compared to your competitors. As those who work with me will confirm, I am a huge proponent of mystery shopping, the excellent marketing strategy in which you "pose" as a consumer or business professional to gain valuable insights regarding various topics, including the competition.

The Mystery

In addition to trying to obtain competitor information from local business groups, be a proactive mystery shopper by contacting the competition directly. You can ask them how they are different; "Why are you more qualified or different than other salespeople?" You'll get information about how they approach clients and how you can do better. You can also ask what they think about you; "I have heard Sam Smith is particularly good at the leasing business. What do you think?" This may give you some very interesting information about how you are perceived in the market.

For example, I have contacted realtors and asked, "I need the names of five top loan originators; who can you suggest and why?" Obviously, I want to be included on their referral list and the information they provide is always helpful.

You can make similar calls. Talk to business leaders and others to gain some useful information regarding local competitors. Explain that you are looking for a realtor, insurance advisor, or car salesperson. When they suggest a few names, ask why they are referring those people. For example: "Why do you think he is the best for a small business loan? Why does she impress you as an exceptional insurance advisor? Would you use him as a realtor and why?" The responses you receive should give you a better idea of the competitors' positive features and whether or not it is worthwhile to make adjustments to your own profile. Obviously, some people will be more willing to provide this feedback than others.

You may also be able to use some of the information to sell your strengths against the competition. There may be techniques your competitors are doing better than you. It doesn't hurt to adopt what they're doing and put your own spin on it. Improve on what they're offering and you'll often gain a leg up on the competition.

If your overall evaluation indicates that you have an outstanding reputation as a salesperson, and that the way you perceive yourself is in line with customers' opinions, you are a step ahead of many others. Congratulations and you can skip the following chapter.

Of course, I really don't think you should miss reading the next several pages. Realizing how my own differentiation has evolved during the last decade, I know that even the best salespeople can benefit from some type of fine-tuning and improvement in their ability to effectively showcase their image.

Chapter Seven
Emphasizing Your Difference:
Time for an Identity Change?

It takes many good deeds to build a good reputation, and only one bad one to lose it. - Benjamin Franklin

Today or one day soon you may, perhaps from reading this book, come to a very uncomfortable realization. You've surveyed your customers and done a self-analysis as I stressed in the previous chapter and determined that you do not stand out in the crowd.

You may find you are indistinguishable from the sales professionals in your market and that your reputation needs a bit of polishing in order to be distinctive.

Prospects may have the wrong perception of you as a salesperson, or they may not be able to define you at all. While they may appreciate you on an individual level, consider how difficult it is to set yourself apart from competitors in your clients' eyes.

Establishing Your Difference

You may need to strengthen the "differentiators" that separate you from all of the other salespeople in your field. What are the key areas that will make people want to do business with you?

It could be that you only need to make a few slight changes, altering the way you represent yourself. Or, you might benefit from adding a special area of expertise or some other distinguishing feature to set yourself apart.

Actually creating a new sales identity will take a little extra time. Start by evaluating a few of the elements with which you are most comfortable. For example, you may decide your customers are especially receptive to extra service, which could involve making home deliveries and offering educational materials. I am reminded of the story of a man who sold tractor parts in a small rural town in Michigan.

One wall in his shop had giant letters written on it proclaiming "World's Greatest Farmers." Underneath he had the photos of each of his customers smiling with their new tractor or farm equipment they had purchased from him.

His nephew, who now works for me, once told me people would often buy from him just because they wanted their picture on the wall, even though the tractor supply company the next town over had the item cheaper. It seems like a small gesture, but it was one of those extra service elements. The tractor salesman was successful because he thought of ways to make his customers feel like they were important.

Being available to your customers is another positive feature; they like knowing that you are willing to answer their questions after hours. This does not necessarily mean you have to be available 24/7, but you should be willing to return phone calls or emails beyond a 9 to 5 schedule. Accessibility is another core element of the Gold Star culture.

You can strengthen your position as an industry expert by expanding your overall understanding of the features of your product or service and customer options. You can read books and trade publications, attend seminars, or even pursue an MBA degree to enhance your knowledge. You can share your expertise with customers during discussions and by providing them with educational materials about your particular products and services.

Another way to set yourself apart is to get involved. Do your best to become active in your community. Donate products, offer contests, charity fundraisers, and other events that let people see the human side of you. A friend who owned a gym once told me he lacked any significant sales success until he decided to throw a fundraiser for the local high school athletic department. He went to the coaches at the school and offered to donate his old equipment to the school so they could have a weight room. It made a big difference in his future sales efforts.

Plan of Action

Create a detailed action plan describing how you intend to develop or enhance your differentiation, outlining the primary steps and a timeline. List five or more actions you can implement right away and another five that may take longer to initiate.

If you are uncertain about which areas you should emphasize, I suggest that you first focus on knowledge and service. People will generally seek a salesperson they believe knows the most about the product or service and who is most concerned with their overall welfare.

Your points of differentiation must have substance. I have seen many salespeople emphasizing that they are "The Most Experienced," or "Offering the Best Service in Town," without backing up their claims. Carefully plan how you will develop your differentiation, and make sure it represents what you truly can deliver.

An Evolving Process

Salespeople don't necessarily maintain a single point of distinction. Your differentiation can evolve over time as you gradually refine your focus, based upon your professional experiences that coincide with your clients' evolving needs. My early point of difference was high volume at a discount. I felt that in order to develop a strong base of customers as soon as possible, I had to create a reputation as a loan originator who could provide a wide range of product options at the best available rates. I am sure many of my first customers would have described me as: "The one who really knows what he is talking about and will give you the best options and lowest available rates… and who talks very fast."

I later realized that prospects can change their perception of salespeople simply by appearance. I recall an interesting experience when I was striving to develop a relationship with a top executive at a leading company in our area. Of course, I was convinced that he would not only give me his immediate business (a very large loan) but continue to refer clients on an ongoing basis. Our previous communication was handled very successfully over the phone; then one day he stopped by to meet me. We talked for a few minutes and he left. I never heard from him again. It seems that I had impressed him with my knowledge during our several phone conversations, but when he saw how young I was and that I was working in a closet-sized office, he changed his perception of me as a salesperson.

As I became more successful and confident in my sales abilities, I developed a reputation as being exceptionally knowledgeable, available to clients, providing customers with the best options, great service, and at the best available rates.

Let Them Know

Once you have determined how you wish to be perceived by customers and others, it is critical that you let them in on the secret. If appropriate, you need to stress your point of distinction on your website, Facebook page, email tag lines, and other places. You can highlight customer testimonials – comments about why they think you are the best – in various promotional materials.

It will take extra time to convince prospects that you are highly knowledgeable, impressing them during sales presentations and other opportunities. During the last decade, I have devoted a great deal of time to acquainting customers with the various facets of home finance, so that they eventually come to recognize me as an expert who will always provide the answers to their specific needs. Salespeople can also demonstrate their expertise by holding weekend workshops and office sales presentations. Noting licenses, degrees, and professional designations on business cards, promotional materials, email signatures, and website pages can further illustrate your knowledge and experience.

Testimonials

Testimonials are powerful marketing tools. Ask your best customers to write a few sentences about one or more of your distinguishing capabilities, if possible giving them samples of other testimonials to use as a guide. Make sure the testimonials they provide are specific. You need customers and others to comment on key areas at which you actually excel, rather than making general summaries that you are "a good salesman."

I once attended a sales seminar where the lecturer interrupted his speech by asking everyone in the theater to leave the room. It was a 500 person auditorium so it took a few minutes to do. We all took a 10-minute break and waited for him to invite us back in. Once he did, we walked in to a theater of darkness. When the house lights came up, the place was littered with information promoting the fake company (Acme Tools) that he was using as an example. Banners had been draped from the ceiling. Flyers covered the seats. Signs had been taped to the wall.

There were balloons and confetti and perhaps most amusingly, even the speaker himself was wearing a sign over his shoulders.

The point he was making was that you need to aggressively brand yourself as to your points of distinction. You need to be visible to your audience. The more ways you can reach your audience, the better chance they will remember you when they are in need of that new car, computer, knife set, or whatever else you are marketing.

It may take time to refocus, to find the ideal way to distinguish yourself from other salespeople. However, it will make a major difference in your longevity as a top producer.

Chapter Eight

Make the Sale: Remember to Close the Door

I have never worked a day in my life without selling. If I believe in something, I sell it, and I sell it hard.
- Estée Lauder

If you list the most critical parts of the sale, it should start with one bold statement:

Close!

This means you need to complete the transaction, to make the sale. Most of us can probably recall an occasion when a prospective customer left our office or store without purchasing, leaving us to wonder if we did something wrong. You may be friendly, knowledgeable, and provide great customer service. However, if you do not have a high closing ratio, you will never be one of your industry's best.

While there are other considerations to being a sales superstar, we are ultimately graded on our production; how many products or service contracts we sell each month, quarter, and year.

In *The ABC of Sales*, I emphasized the importance of knowing how to close effectively. Here is a brief recap of the basics, which as a professional salesperson you should already know:

• **Analyze your closing ratio.** You have to know how effective you are so you can take the steps to improve. By tracking the number of prospects you meet and the number of actual sales, you'll know how successful you are as a closer. Your analysis can also note the types of customers, whether for example they are "serious" buyers or "tire kickers."

• **Listen carefully to the customer's needs.** You must find out what is most important to them, whether it is price, features, service, or any combination of these. They will often tell you exactly what they need or prefer in order to close the sale.

• **Ask the tough questions.** Whether selling automobiles or computers, you have to ask questions that reveal the prospect's intentions, the likelihood they are going to buy. "What is the reason you are looking at (whatever they are considering buying)? What was the problem with the previous product? Are you ready to buy today?"

• **Answer prospects' objections.** Practice various scenarios so that you can respond to their concerns about the product, service, or other issues. You should develop a master list of objections and the appropriate responses. If you've been listening carefully, you'll know what each customer's objections are. You should be so adept at answering the typical objections that you can respond in almost any situation.

Someone reminded me about the time I was in a serious phone conversation with a prospect who was concerned about a few key areas of her loan. I answered every one of the questions to her satisfaction, while simultaneously moving a soccer ball around my office. I certainly took her concerns seriously, but had become so experienced dealing with the usual objections that it was almost "second nature."

Ask to Know

Practice your own Q&A routine. Your informal script should start with "What brings you here today?" You should be able to learn if your prospects are motivated to purchase right then, or if they are in a fact-finding mode. Each question can lead you into a different path of either closing quickly or creating a positive impression so that they will ask for you when they return for the actual purchase. For example, if they respond, "My television stopped working last night," you can be confident they are in the mood to buy and you can go in that direction. On the other hand, if they say "I have heard about your new model, and I'm curious about how it differs from what we already have," you will need more time to educate them.

• **Ask for the business.** If necessary, confirm that you have provided all the necessary information about the specific product or service and that you have answered any remaining questions. Asking for the business seems like a simple point, but it's one that many salespeople delay unnecessarily.

• **Overcome mental roadblocks.** Some of the
most natural salespeople are nervous about closing
the sale because they lack confidence, are afraid to ask
for the money, are worried about saying the wrong
thing, or are otherwise concerned about this vital
part of the sales process. Most customers can sense
this and may back away or seek another salesperson.
You've got to get over such fears right away, or else
you'll never make it in sales.

• **Move quickly for unexpected opportunities.**
There will be occasions when a prospect has encountered difficulty with his or her current salesperson and
wants to close right away. You need to be ready to act.
I recall when a celebrity photographer called me from
his hotel room in Florida, where he and his family
were stuck because their current lender wasn't able to
close their loan as promised. I was extremely busy at
the time, but didn't want to lose the opportunity to
help them. We first talked at 9 p.m. on a Friday night
and I told him not to worry. Of course, I had to call
my support team in that weekend, but by Monday
afternoon we had closed their loan. He was definitely
happy and has since referred a number of his friends
and associates to me.

• **Don't Be Pushy.** Certainly the most sensitive
point is when the buyer is about ready to make a
decision. Some salespeople derail the sale by raising
unnecessary issues, or worse, pushing too hard and

irritating the customer. Sometimes the customer is ready to purchase but a nervous salesman is afraid of the silence and keeps talking, inadvertently raising a concern the customer hadn't anticipated. If you've already provided the appropriate information and answered all of their questions, there is absolutely no reason to keep pushing. In fact, they should be pushing you to buy the product.

Assuming Control

One of the closing strategies that may take a little longer to master is being in control of the sales process. That does not mean you are domineering or inflexible in your approach. It means that you are able to direct the focus and pace of the transaction to the desired outcome.

Some salespeople have a tendency to let their customers get sidetracked during their conversations. They start the discussion with the prospect explaining what she is looking for, her budget, and other relevant details, but 10 minutes later they are talking about the upcoming football game, the winter weather, the economy or other topics that don't necessarily help achieve a successful close. Never allow your presentation to derail.

Of course, I'm not saying that your customer conversations have to be all business; there is definitely time for "off topic" chit chat. One of the best ways to develop rapport with clients is to converse about their personal areas of interest. The key is to keep the proper balance and to always steer the discussion back to their original intent of obtaining a desired product or service.

Most salespeople develop their customer presentation gradually, making adjustments based on prospect feedback and other factors. The essentials are the same: learning the customer's needs, asking questions to see how your product or service can help them solve a challenge or satisfy a specific need, answering objections, and confirming their readiness to purchase.

I.D. the Decision Makers

I've had some enlightening conversations with various salespeople who have shared some of their observations and experiences regarding customers who seem indecisive, often because they aren't the sole decision maker. In order to be certain about who you are dealing with, it's necessary to do some basic research. You want to determine whether or not they are a true potential buyer, and if there are others involved. Doing so could save you an unnecessary delay in closing a sale.

Hopefully, you already know who makes the decisions for all of your corporate clients. For example, selling a new computer system may only require the signature of a purchasing manager, or it may take a committee's approval. If you sense your immediate contact is having difficulty getting the purchase contract approved, quickly suggest that you and he get input from another source, who might have additional details regarding a longer buying cycle or other critical issues.

Confirm Your Buyers

The next time you have a prospect who seems overly positive about making a major transaction, determine if there are other people involved in the decision process. Of course, you want to do this subtly so as not to irritate your prime contact. Ask someone else you know at the company ("I've been talking with Sam about your need for a new line of computers and we're planning on delivery next month..."), which may prompt some feedback. Alternatively, you could ask another salesperson at your firm to see if they have information that contradicts or otherwise clarifies the customer's enthusiasm.

There are other instances where you have to confer with everyone involved in a potential purchase to see why they differ on essential points. Much of my business is conducted on the phone, but this can have its disadvantages in certain situations. I recall several instances where a husband or wife made the initial call to discuss a loan. They were very enthusiastic and discussed their short and long-term goals. Then a few days later, one spouse would call to question a decision or point that the other person had made. That's when would I ask them both to come in at the same time, so we could be sure we are all moving in the same direction. You should consider doing this same thing, whether you are selling computers, cars, or furniture. For example, if your young buyer and her parents are purchasing a new laptop for college and there is uncertainty about who the actual decision maker is or a lack of agreement about cost, features, or any other significant point, you need to "sit them all down" to clarify everyone's role and clear up any confusion before proceeding.

Most people who work with me will confirm that I am relentless in my pursuit of closing a sale. I don't enjoy having a strong referral prospect walk away without deciding to use my services. However, I also recognize the importance of treating all customers fairly. Once I see that someone isn't ready to buy, I don't push them away or appear disinterested, because I know if I treat them well, they may return later and also refer others. Asking questions to evaluate a customer's readiness to buy lets me strike a careful balance between pushing for the sale and the need to remain friendly and not rush them.

But none of us can forget that at the end of the day, week, and month, it is the sales report that matters. To be a sales superstar, you need to perfect your own formula for timely closings, and every salesperson has to assess the amount of time they are willing to spend with non-committed prospects.

Also, you may consider yourself a master closer, but it is easy to get stale, so take time to refresh your approach.

Remember the great words of Donald Trump: "People get caught up in wonderful, eye-catching pitches, but they don't do enough to close the deal. It's no good if you don't make the sale. Even if your foot is in the door or you bring someone into a conference room, you don't win the deal unless you actually get them to sign on the dotted line."

Chapter Nine

Hire an Assistant: You Need One to Get There

One of the jobs of a manager is to instill confidence, pump confidence into your people. And when you've got somebody who's raring to go and you can smell it and feel it, give 'em that shot. - Jack Welch

I f you want to be a sales superstar, you will need:

An Assistant

You can certainly be successful without having an assistant, but you shouldn't work solo if you intend to break through the inevitable sales volume barriers on your way to becoming a superstar.

If you don't currently have someone to help with routine tasks, there will come a day when you probably will need help. Otherwise you will become consumed with paperwork and other administrative details, your production will level off, and you will be unable to meet with any more prospects. Having an assistant can be the difference between decent success and superstar success.

A critical part of developing a support system is knowing where your time is best spent. Successful, aspiring sales superstars must be rainmakers who bring in the business. Your focus should be on developing effective marketing campaigns, generating new leads, meeting with prospects, and closing sales. If you spend too much time on miscellaneous details, you could easily end up becoming a part-time salesperson and a part-time assistant.

An assistant enables you to focus on revenue-generating activity, to avoid the work you dislike or aren't particularly good at, to become better organized, and even to take vacations knowing your business can flourish. You have to consider an assistant as a profit center rather than an expense. In addition to freeing up more of your time to concentrate on sales and marketing, there are even instances when an assistant will contribute more directly to the sales bottom line. For example, I have witnessed numerous situations when extra attention to detail or special service by one of our assistants so impressed prospects that it made them more inclined to do business with us. When someone who desperately needs an assistant tells me they can't afford the expense, I insist that "You can't afford not to have one."

Knowing When

There is no simple formula for knowing when to hire an assistant, since timing will vary depending on a variety of factors. The first step is to determine that you actually require additional support. When one of our salespeople enthusiastically exclaims "I'm so busy, I've got to have an assistant," I give them the five minute "Are you sure?" talk. I ask a few key questions: Are you already working a long week? Are you taking long lunches and/or spending unnecessary time in meetings? Are you buried in paperwork? If they are already working at peak efficiency, I usually encourage them to find an assistant. If not, I suggest they wait until they are working at the optimum level.

Calculate Non-Sales Time

Keep a daily log of how much time you spend on non-sales activity: writing reports, processing orders, filling out call logs, and related activity. Doing this over a two- or three-month period should give you a good idea of how much time you spend on work that does not directly contribute to your sales volume. If you are in a retail environment where most of your time should be devoted to customer contact, keep track of how much time you are actually selling versus breaks, interaction with other salespeople, and meetings.

In the mortgage lending profession, closing 100 or more loans per year is often cited as the "tipping point," when loan originators hit the wall and are unable to produce more without some type of assistance. Certainly this varies, depending on a salesperson's work schedule and other factors.

An obvious sign that you are in desperate need of an assistant is when your work week greatly exceeds 40 hours. We're not talking about an "appropriate" level of overtime or even home office follow-up activity. I mean if you're at the office 60 hours or so on a regular basis, it's probably time to consider the options or risk eventual burnout.

I hired an assistant after about a year as a loan originator, and I should have done so earlier. I had been doing a variety of chores that were necessary but certainly not adding to my production. I was answering all of the phones, processing loans, ordering supplies and handling a variety of other tasks that weren't directly contributing to my sales goals, and I became concerned that I wouldn't be able to achieve my aggressive volume targets. Once I shifted some of that responsibility to an assistant, my volume increased dramatically.

Consider the Options

You may be fortunate enough to work for a company that understands the value of providing its successful salespeople with support, based on their current and projected production. Many companies contribute a portion or all of the salary for a top salesperson's assistant. But if that perk is not available, you will need to make this investment yourself.

This is a great time to think out of the box. There are several ways you can obtain assistance, whether you are in a retail environment or in a professional services or office situation. For example:

• **Hire a part-time assistant,** someone who can work with you or offsite. You can do this on your own or through a virtual assistant firm. While you won't have on-site support with a virtual assistant, you'll be able to work with qualified people at reasonable rates. Talk to other salespeople who have gone this route to get their opinions on what to look for, the interview process, and other insights.

• **Enlist friends or family members.** Ask a friend, neighbor, or relative to help out. They can compile lists of family/friend prospects, compile marketing materials and handle other tasks.

• **Share an assistant.** Hire one helper for two or more salespeople. You only have to cover part of the salary and this will give you an idea about how to work with an assistant.

The Right Choice

It is important to determine whether you want someone who will be a long-term assistant or one who will eventually grow into a different role on your team. Some people enjoy performing only assistant-type tasks, whereas others require the potential of greater responsibilities in the future.

The Gold Star hiring and training program generally focuses on developing applicants who have the ability to become a loan originator or assume another position within the company, rather than those whose primary goal is to continue as an assistant. Angie Fant, my second assistant, was instrumental in helping me significantly expand my production; in one month alone, she worked long hours to help close 181 loans. She later took on other responsibilities and has been with Gold Star in different capacities for a decade. I am also seeking younger people who are enthusiastic and relatively easy to train. I want someone who is willing to work long hours when necessary, and who is able to think independently. Obviously, finding the right assistant will depend on your personal and company preferences. "One size fits all" does not apply to hiring assistants.

I am not a big believer in the use of written tests to select the best candidate, although I understand that many organizations consider them a vital employment tool. I do like to find out how interviewees handle a challenge, and for this reason I ask them to "make a sale" at the end of our regular interview. I will tell them to sell me a coffee pot, book, or other nearby item. This is a great way to see if they have a basic understanding of the sales profession, and to gauge how they deal with stress. Even though your assistant won't immediately be required to actually sell, they will be responsible for talking with customers, dealing with objections, and handling related tasks. This will give you greater insights than relying solely on their rehearsed responses to "What is your greatest strength?" and "What is your favorite job?" I certainly don't make a decision based on how they make an impromptu sale, but it does provide another informative dimension to their interview.

The Transition

I know that some salespeople like to have assistants handle many of their personal errands, such as shopping and arranging for car maintenance. I prefer to have my assistants focus primarily on work-related areas; otherwise, they can easily become disenchanted with their role. Assistants need to see that they are making a valuable contribution and that there is a definite potential for a promising career.

Your Shadow

It is a good idea to have your new assistant "shadow" you to get a full idea of what you do and why their work is important to your success. Too often, salespeople hand their new assistants a stack of paper to file and then leave them alone for days. They don't have to be sitting at the next desk as mine are; just make sure they see the "big picture" of your work. Have them accompany you on a sales call or listen while you talk with customers on the phone. You'll need to have an "assistant development" plan in place so that they see you don't do everything "on the fly."

Some salespeople find it difficult to work with an assistant because it interferes with their normal routine. It's true that time spent training an assistant can be inconvenient during the first few months, when you have to spend extra time answering questions and reviewing their work. It usually takes three to four months to properly train an assistant, after which it should become a smooth running system.

Others find delegating to be a major challenge. They are adamant that, "No one does it as well as I can; I am afraid I'll lose touch with my customers." This feeling is natural. After acquiring your first customers, you spent time and effort making sure to respond to their future needs, and they have become accustomed to you answering each phone call and handling every aspect of their purchases. You're convinced they'll miss you.

To overcome "delegate phobia," start gradually reassigning some of the "unwanted" tasks. Introduce your longtime customers to your assistant as a "key part of our team." Explain that having an assistant will enable you to provide even better service, and that you will remain involved in their future transactions. If appropriate, schedule semi-annual calls to reassure your most important customers that you haven't lost touch.

Obviously, many salespeople – including those in retail store settings – will not have the option of working side-by-side with their assistants, who will most likely be off-site. There are still ways you can maintain regular contact. For example, meet for coffee or lunch to provide background information about your products or services and share highlights of your sales activity. You can also exchange emails or text messages during your breaks.

You may decide you don't have the time or resources to devote to training and managing an assistant now. If you are unsure, it is probably wise to wait a while. However, don't be too conservative in your approach to seeking some type of assistance. I would not be nearly as successful today without having taken advantage of the support of my previous and current assistants.

Chapter Ten
Pay Attention to Customers: Hold on Tight

We see our customers as invited guests to a party, and we are the hosts. It's our job every day to make every important aspect of the customer experience a little bit better.
- Jeff Bezos, CEO, Amazon.com

A recipe for short-term sales success is to concentrate solely on new prospects and ignore your past customers. It is a mistake that many salespeople make.

The fact is, creating loyal, lifelong customers will help ensure a steady business on which you can count. While this might seem so incredibly simple, it is a guiding principle that all salespeople should follow. Statistics show it is easier to sell something to someone who has already purchased from you.

Developing a base of repeat customers is also financially rewarding. According to one study, a five percent increase in customer retention can increase your profits by 30 to 50 percent.

When I started as a mortgage originator, I was intent on collecting as many new customers as possible, because I was sure that was the way to make sales quickly. But before too long I began to realize the wisdom of having repeat customers. I recall the light bulb turning on when a past customer called one busy morning and said "You did such a great job with our recent purchase that we want to use you from now on." This provided first-hand proof of the benefit of maintaining a loyal group of past customers. I actually remember thinking, "I am going to make this a top priority," and I have done just that throughout my sales career.

First Impressions

Prospective customers initially come to you for very specific reasons, including product availability, price, your location, or a strong referral from a friend or associate. They generally return for future purchases because you have made a positive first impression and then remain visible, or even offer additional post-sale support. They will remember and appreciate what you have done, so why would they want to start over with a new salesperson?

Your relationship with customers begins or ends with the first meeting or phone conversation. You must do everything possible to ensure that it is a pleasant and productive experience. This means listening carefully to customers' concerns, answering questions, providing solutions, and generally making the transaction seem like an easy process, so that they say, "What a great decision to buy from this professional." You must come across in such a manner that is genuine and truly connects with the prospect.

If, on the other hand, it seems you are disinterested, unable to satisfactorily answer their questions, or can't provide the item they want to purchase, you will definitely lose a few points.

Gold Star makes it a point to impress our new customers from the minute they enter our offices. For example, visitors are greeted by a cheerful receptionist and then escorted to a comfortable welcome area. Hearing nearby salespeople and support staff enthusiastically conferring with other customers and prospects gives them a sense of the office's positive energy. Individual awards earned by some of our top producers are prominently displayed on the wall so customers know they are about to meet with some of the industry's best.

Dissect Your Presentation

Take time to analyze your sales "pitch," your first interaction with new customers. Do you listen carefully and ask the right questions? Do you spend sufficient time addressing all of their concerns? Objectively critique your approach and see if you can improve it.

Whether this first contact is a personal meeting or phone discussion, my focus is always on the prospect's needs. I ask about their current situation, future plans, goals, family, dreams, and any concerns they might have. People appreciate being educated about products and services as long as it helps them make a decision, so I am certain to highlight areas about which they may not be familiar.

Then I stop talking and listen to them. I genuinely care about their welfare, and I believe they can sense that.

Your customers need to see that you are really concerned with what is important to them. "Walking in their shoes" and empathizing with their situation is probably the most important element of a solid first impression. This may mean that you suggest they only need a more inexpensive model or basic service, which won't necessarily endear you to the sales manager, but the customer will remember you for your sincere interest in their well-being, and they will return to do business with you. And they will send you many referrals.

It is also necessary to consider any personal habits that might interfere with the customer-salesperson interaction. We all have our own likes and dislikes regarding the sales experience. Personally, I don't enjoy being oversold when I am making a purchase. It is so easy to tell the difference between a salesperson educating me about various products or services and one with an overbearing attitude indicating that the sale is his overriding goal.

Of course, the transaction itself must be as trouble-free as you can make it. At Gold Star, that means keeping the customer apprised of major developments throughout the process and closing the loan on time or early. Apply the same concept to your profession. Is the product in stock? Do customers typically have a lengthy wait before being helped? Can the sale itself be completed as quickly as the customer wants?

You can also look for other ways to have a positive first impact. For example, talk to your sales manager about offering refreshments or a play area for children. Maybe you could provide educational handouts such as "Ten Quick Tips on Getting the Most From Your (Product)."

The Multi-Generational Benefits

My upfront goal with every customer is to establish a permanent relationship, and one way I accomplish this is by emphasizing that I don't consider them a "sale." I explain that my priority is addressing their immediate needs. But equally important, I emphasize that I want to create a bond whereby I will be able to assist them and family members for all of their future financial services-related plans. I make it clear I am truly interested in having them as "customers for life," and that I will go to great lengths to achieve this.

I have many customers for whom I have done multiple loans over the last 15 years. I have also been fortunate to assist some of their children and parents. I remember the satisfaction I felt the first time a repeat customer asked me to help a son who wanted to purchase his first home. I had earned the customer's trust, so he felt comfortable recommending me to the most important people in his life – his children.

A key aspect of the multi-generational approach is advising customers when you can offer products and programs that may benefit their family members. For example, insurance advisors can emphasize student auto coverage or life insurance policies designed for older adults. Loan originators are able to provide seniors with reverse mortgages. Computer salespeople have the option to introduce "back to school laptop or tablet specials" for high school and college students. Car sales representatives might offer newly-licensed drivers a "safest car on the road driving program" or a "New Year leasing bonus for senior drivers."

Survey Their Satisfaction

Make sure you attempt to obtain feedback from your customers about their experience, especially after their first purchase. Basic questions include: "Were you satisfied with your purchase? Why? Will you purchase from me again? Why? How can I improve my service?" A brief written survey (keep it brief!) will provide the most objective responses. You can also ask customers or prospects about their previous experiences with competitors. What did they like or dislike?

It requires a little imagination and management's support to initiate such potentially rewarding programs, but they can strengthen your relationship with existing customers and develop ties with both younger and older generations.

It does not take too much effort to make a positive first impression. But then you must continue reminding customers that you want to serve them in the future.

25+2 Ways to Enhance Your Sales Performance

As recommended by the faculty, College of Management and MBA students of Cleary University in Ann Arbor, Michigan.

Put the right team together for the task. It is essential to take the time to network, recruit and interview each individual team player to ensure that all the roles necessary for success are represented.

Relationship building – don't burn bridges. This is perhaps the most critical skill you need to be successful. Don't play the solo game; stick to the golden rule of helping others. This means building the right bridges with key contacts and keeping them!

Situational awareness – understand the 3-6 month cycle vs. 2-3 year cycle. Strategic planning is essential, but you also must attend to the time factor in different types of sales situations. Because it takes much longer to close on a sale of some products or services, you need to adjust your planning, especially as you learn to handle new lines.

Continually practice positive thinking. Set the PACE – Positive Attitudes Change Everything. Put another way, if you believe you will fail – you probably will. Start every day with an "I will succeed" and an "I can do this" mindset.

Overcome and underscore the objections. This goes back to being prepared. If you anticipate objections, you will know how to deal effectively with them when they come up. We often emphasize the strategies of "Kung Fu Selling." Among other ideas, this concept suggests that a salesperson can capture the energy of the sales relationship by effectively absorbing the customer's questions and redirecting the objections. The buyer's objection is dissolved in such a way that he will want to buy the product or service.

Create unique competitive and comparative advantages; create barriers to entry for your competitors. Answer the question "Why will people want to do business with you?" Such benefits as excellent service, availability, and uniqueness will help ensure that customers think of you as their first choice.

Make it better and cheaper. Every good entrepreneur knows that quality, price, and timely delivery always equal success. As a salesperson, you may not have control over all of these factors. However, always be sure to accent the most positive combination your company offers.

Start with the close, not with the pitch. Customers expect a sales pitch in the beginning. Start with why they should buy your product, or service. For example, sell the sizzle, not the steak.

Let passion pressure you to outperform your peers. This relates back to selling what you believe in. Customers and prospects can generally sense that you believe in your product and truly enjoy what you do.

Anticipate customer needs to eliminate objections. If customers do not need what you offer, why should they buy it? Work hard enough to understand how your product or service will improve the life of your prospect, and there is a good chance that the prospect will become a customer.

Knowledge of your marketplace is critical. Knowing your marketplace is essential if you are to offer a competitive price. Do your research by checking with clients, vendors and others who have worked with or are aware of your competitors.

Sell your differences and not your similarities. You need to show potential customers how you stand out from your competitors. Create a list of unique things about you as a salesperson that will make your customers appreciate you.

Know thyself. Know yourself well enough to do what you do well. How can you influence others if you do not know who YOU are? Understand your overall motivation, along with your strengths and weaknesses.

Hone your verbal and written skills. A poorly presented or badly written proposal illustrates lackluster professionalism, and you will be judged accordingly. Do your homework, spend time developing your presentation and then make the best possible delivery.

Become an expert in reading body language. Nonverbal communication is 94 percent of all communication. Watch your prospect's facial expressions and hand gestures. You'll find clues of their agreement, frustration, buy-in, etc.

Light up your emotional intelligence. A gifted salesperson knows how to empathize and establish a rapport. Spend time trying to understand your customer's unique situation and think carefully about what's important to them. Let this understanding guide your conversations with customers.

Harness your listening powers. The best of the best seem to always be masterful listeners. Ask the right questions, but then let your customer do most of the talking. Capture this quality and you will see your sales soar.

Enhance your attitude. Attitude is altitude. The more dynamic and engaging, the higher you will go. Always show perseverance, dedication, and excitement.

Leverage the Internet to become the industry expert. Entrepreneurs in the 21st century know the value of e-commerce. We are working in a rapidly changing environment, and you will get left behind if you don't know how to use these fundamental tools to your advantage.

Recognize the pain points, know the solutions, and satisfy their needs. There are many components to making a successful sale, but these three are essential. What are the problems that keep the customer from completing the transaction? How can you work with them to eliminate these barriers?

Be quick on your feet. Top performers can always solve the toughest problems, even if they don't have the immediate solutions. The trick is to be competent in the moment. Always respond quickly to a prospect's questions, telephone message, or email.

Navigate the variables. Take every detail into account when establishing your goals. Consider the potential challenges and how they might create opportunities.

Measure and review, then make changes where needed. Remember the MAD cycle (Measure, Analyze, and Decide). Do not be afraid to change course and be flexible each day to recognize new developments.

Fish where the fish are. Try to talk to people who are willing to listen to you. It is fine to develop new audiences, but be sure to focus on those you believe will be the most receptive to your message.

Send the right message. Make sure that your message is on target and is received the right way. You want prospects to be "on the same page" as to product/service benefits, price, and other critical details.

Know how to take a risk. When a sales opportunity knocks on your door, smile and take it. An entrepreneurial and bold attitude can help you become a top producer.

Get focused and stay focused! Believe in what you want to achieve – see it, hold it, and rarely will you be blindsided. It may be difficult to remain on your course, but being committed to your goals will help ensure that you don't head in the wrong direction.

(Cleary University: www.cleary.edu)

Chapter Eleven

Follow-up Is Crucial:
You Can at Least Send Them a Birthday Card

The need to communicate effectively with your customers will come up again and again. - Bill Gates

You can smile, ask the right questions, listen carefully, and provide a great product at the most reasonable price…and your customer may still go elsewhere to make the next purchase.

When this happens, it is most likely because even though you created an excellent first impression during the initial transaction, you subsequently made a major sales error; you neglected to stay in contact with your customer after the sale.

If you have any doubts about the importance of customer follow-up, consider this startling statistic that has been attributed to the real estate profession. One year after their home purchase, more than 80 percent of new homeowners don't recall the name of their real estate agent.

That is an alarming figure. It means that salespeople may provide excellent service, yet just one year later that customer does not remember them. When the customer wishes to make a future purchase or has an opportunity to make a referral, the original sales-person may be overlooked.

While this survey stat was originally based on the real estate profession, I'm certain that it applies to salespeople in numerous other industries. The actual percentage of customers who can't remember their salespeople will vary, but the basic, sad fact is prob-ably accurate. Many salespeople take customers for granted and then seem surprised when they decide to buy from a competitor.

There is another set of amazing statistics that underscores the value of paying attention to your customers and prospects. In a survey of why busi-nesses lose customers (from FollowUpSuccess.com), it was explained that a few basic reasons are because the customer dies (1%), moves away (3%), forms other relationships (5%), leaves over competitive reasons (9%) or becomes dissatisfied with the product (14%). However, an incredible 68% stop buying your prod-uct or service because of an indifferent attitude shown by you or someone at your company. They think you don't care about them.

A major reason for this feeling of neglect is that the salesperson hasn't taken the time to follow-up with the customer. For example, 48% of salespeople don't follow-up with a customer or prospect, 25% stop after making a second contact and only 12% make more than three contacts.

Whether those worrisome stats apply more to prospects than regular customers, the point is clear. In order to have "top of the mind awareness" among those with whom you want to do business, you have to stay in touch. You must send a letter, holiday or birthday card, or make a call to see how the customer is enjoying the new product or service.

Consistent Contact

Statistics confirm that people generally need to be exposed to you (and your product) multiple times in order to be ready to purchase. The Marketing Rule of Seven is an old concept which says that your prospective buyer needs to hear or see your marketing message at least seven times before they will purchase from you.

Of course, some salespeople are fortunate to be in regular contact with customers they visit on normal sales calls. They have an opportunity to obtain regular "face time" with key contacts. However, many of us need to make an effort to follow-up on a consistent basis by:

• **Mailing a flier regarding a new product/program or other newsworthy topic.** Be cautious about overloading them with every new product announcement.

• **Sending holiday greetings and birthday cards.** Mark your calendar or use something like Boomerang for Gmail to schedule customized messages.

• **Providing educational materials about your specific industry,** such as "Calculating Your Future Mortgage Payment," "Insurance Facts & Figures," "Auto Leasing vs. Purchasing" and so on. Maybe you're selling a new weight-loss product. You could send them a brochure on "10 Ways to Lose 10 Pounds Fast." You are providing information that helps them.

• **Sending an article related to something in which they're interested.** It could be about one of their hobbies or a family-related topic.

• **Tweeting about something of interest.** Once you are social media savvy, you can send customers something that would be helpful. You can even connect them with others who have similar interests.

• **Texting your message.** According to a study by Opus Research, short message service (SMS) marketing results in more targeted promotions and, in turn, more effective results. 97% of SMS messages are opened, compared to any other form of contact. The great thing is that you can schedule these text messages on certain days, such as birthdays.

I send customers quarterly letters on various topics and include a short handwritten note encouraging them to contact me for their annual mortgage checkup. They may gloss over (or totally ignore) the letter, but most are probably interested in the note because even though it is copied, it appears handwritten. A customized item will usually get better results than an e-blasted form letter.

Education is Key

People generally appreciate receiving educational information. Complement your sales and product offering mailers with fliers and brochures that highlight new applications for their product, or a technology or process that may be of interest. In addition, you can send information that helps your customers in other ways. For example, email a reminder to "Turn Your Clock Back This Weekend," or during Fire Safety Week, mail a one-page notice of "15 Home Fire Safety Tips." While these may have nothing to do with your product or service, it shows customers you have a genuine concern for them beyond the sale.

I also mail an annual calendar with a reminder about the check-up. We send one of the calendars to the customer's home and another to their workplace, which creates an opportunity for them to tell colleagues why they have chosen to work with me. These are such simple gestures, yet they get a great response and help accomplish my objective of being recognized as their permanent loan originator.

I contact past customers directly six to 10 times a

year. Early in my career, the customer follow-up was even more frequent, but I gradually scaled it back as I learned that too many mailings could actually become irritating to customers. You will need to develop the proper contact schedule for your own customers.

Call Them

You also have several opportunities to talk directly with customers:

• Ask how they are doing and answer questions regarding the product or service.

• Alert them to a sale, special product, or service.

• Introduce your annual "audit" whereby you review how recent changes or new benefits could have a positive effect on their car lease, life insurance policy, computer maintenance program, or other recently purchased product or service.

• Greet them with birthday or anniversary wishes.

Survey

Obviously, some customers will prefer not to receive emails, mailers, or phone calls. I have had very few actually say they did not want to hear from me. However, you may wish to survey your customers to determine their preferences. For example, you can give them a brief form at the conclusion of your first transaction or send an email to learn:

• Are they receptive to receiving updates?

- How often do they wish to be contacted?
- Do they prefer emails, mailers, and/or calls?
- Would they like to receive information about sales, new products, programs, or other useful information? Any other topic?

Beyond the Norm

There are other creative ways to maintain visibility with customers. For example, Gold Star's Concierge Service enables customers to call a prepaid 60-minute 800 number to receive special assistance, including corporate research, travel arrangements, entertainment reservations, and even personal shopping. Customers love this extra bonus. Every time they dial the 800 number, they think of Gold Star and me.

I also provide a Professional Services Referral Directory. This is a database of service providers, including CPAs, financial planners, attorneys, and others in my market that I frequently share with past customers. They know that I verify these contacts' professionalism, and they appreciate this extra attention. This is something most salespeople can easily develop.

Gold Star has held very popular Customer Appreciation Tailgate parties prior to the annual Michigan/ Michigan State football game. This is a great chance to meet and talk to customers with whom we have not had recent contact. This is a corporate event, and I realize most salespeople are not likely to host such a large gathering for their customers, but you could use the idea on a smaller scale, such as a picnic in the park.

There are other "outside the box" steps you can take. For instance, send a coupon for a discount on the customer's next purchase or offer five hours of specialized instruction on the use of their new product. I was definitely impressed when a major car dealer was able to deliver a car directly to my house to purchase, thereby eliminating my need to visit the dealership.

VIP Attention

It may make sense for you to concentrate more of your follow-up activity on repeat customers. Review your database to determine which customers made the most purchases during the last two years. You might want to send them a few additional cards or emails during the year, while still maintaining contact with the rest of your database.

Salespeople may insist they don't have the money or time to stay connected with their past customers. This is usually just an excuse for being too lazy or unaware of how to proceed. Remember the two components of customer follow-up:

1. Do something; and

2. Be consistent.

Know Your Customers

It should seem obvious, but salespeople need to develop a thorough understanding of what motivates their customers to make repeat purchases. The first step is to keep an accurate record of past customer transactions. If possible you should note the type and frequency of purchases each customer has made over the last several years. This will enable you to monitor the type of follow-up for customers who have made several purchases compared to those who are likely to be one-time buyers, and will also provide you with key details you can use when talking with a regular customer.

When a customer calls me, I can quickly check their status on my PC or laptop. While I do have a good memory for customer details, I have found that an online tracking program is an even more efficient way to review a customer's profile. It makes them feel especially good to know that I am so familiar with their preferences and previous purchases. Even if you don't have a PC at your sales "station," you can at least keep a Rolodex or similar file in which you can detail customer buying habits.

You can learn about customer buying patterns in other ways as well. For example, you may have a past customer call to explain that one of your competitors approached them about a special offer on a product or service. This is actually one of my favorite calls to receive. The customer usually wants to talk about the other salesperson's "deal" and seeks my perspective before making a decision. This gives me a chance to highlight my knowledge and interest in helping them, and emphasize why they should continue to do business with me.

All salespeople should make this sort of "Customers for Life" focus a key part of their overall business strategy. You don't want to be one of those whom your customer forgets after the initial sale. Take advantage of the momentum gained by your positive first impressions with customers. Stay in contact. Send a birthday card. Remind them you are still thinking about their needs. If you don't, you will definitely lose some future sales.

Chapter Twelve

Building a Referral Network: One Becomes 25

Referrals aren't given easily. If you don't take the time to establish credibility, you're not going to get the referral. People have to get to know you. They have to feel comfortable with who you are and what you do."
- Ivan Misner

1SC+1Rx2MR=SIV

That is one of my favorite equations. It means 1 Satisfied Customer Plus 1 Referral Times Two More Referrals Equals Steadily Increasing Volume.

Referrals are a cash cow for all superstar salespeople. If you want to know how important referrals are to your success, just do the math. If one customer refers a friend, who then refers a neighbor, who recommends two work associates... You get the idea. Referrals from those people multiply exponentially, and you can suddenly be looking at a major increase in your customer base.

I have had a single customer refer me to more than 20 new customers and their subsequent combined referrals added numerous other sales to my production total.

Top-producing salespeople consider referrals to be the lifeblood of their business. A steady supply of referrals will be a bonus during your busy sales periods, and it will definitely help sustain you during slower times.

Unfortunately, many salespeople are slow to learn about the power of referrals. Perhaps they forget that you generally have to sell "cold" prospects on a reason to use you, while a referred customer generally doesn't need to be convinced. Someone else has already endorsed you as the sales representative to meet their needs.

Evaluate Yourself

Before reading any further, I suggest you do the following evaluation. First, estimate the approximate number of referrals you have received during the last year. Then try to calculate these transactions as a percentage of your total business. In other words, what percent of your total volume is referral based? Don't count the leads you have received from an ad, sales presentation, or website. I am talking about direct referrals from a neighbor, work colleague, or prior customer.

Next, see if you can identify the people who have provided the greatest number of referrals during the same period. You may not be able to get an exact number, but you should have a good idea of the approximate amount of referral business. If you can't come close to determining this important figure, you need to start keeping track today.

Referral Sources

Your most likely sources of referrals are family members, friends and others in your immediate sphere of influence. But there are others with whom you need to connect.

• **Networking Groups:** One of the most effective referral-generating strategies is to join an association dedicated to sharing leads with its members. You can certainly create your own networking group, but it seems more logical to associate with one that is already organized and proven to produce results, such as BNI International, the world's largest networking organization. Of course, there are also online groups, websites, blogs, and other social media resources you can include in your professional network.

Referral Listing

Develop a directory of potential referral sources, including past customers as well as family, members of various professional and community groups you belong to, and others. Make sure that all members of these groups are aware of what you do. Send letters and emails, attend mixers, and offer to speak at meetings. Then keep a record of how many referrals these efforts provide.

• **Niche Referrals:** Niche customer groups can be an especially fertile source of referrals. The people in these groups share common interests and usually rely on each other for support in various areas. They are also generally quite loyal about referring friends and relatives to salespeople who have been especially helpful.

As an inexperienced loan originator, I sought to befriend newly-arrived and other immigrants in a growing Russian community in Ann Arbor, Michigan. I helped many of them find an apartment, obtain a driver's license, and handle other challenging tasks. They trusted me as the "go-to guy," and when anyone needed a mortgage, they were referred to me. Once I established myself, I came to realize how incredibly strong "word of mouth" referral networking is.

To successfully sell to specific ethnic groups, you need to have a basic understanding of their culture and any special ways individuals prefer to make their major purchases. You can begin by asking a few of the more well-known residents to share their insights, along with reading the local newspaper and attending community meetings. Of course, it also helps to speak the language.

In addition to ethnic groups, other loyal niches include law enforcement and fire personnel, PTA organizations, and athletic and band booster groups. At Gold Star, we encourage our salespeople to reach out to diverse groups. For example, one of them has created an effective niche with his local fire department. "It has taken me years to gain their trust, as they 'sit around the firehouse and talk,'" he explained. "That phrase is used frequently between the firemen, which goes to show that they do talk about each other's experiences and what each other is doing. Many firemen have other jobs; for example, they may also be working as realtors, financial planners, or mortgage brokers. They rely on each other for valuable information. As I have slowly built a great rapport with the local departments, word is spreading quickly about how well they are treated, which goes a long way when it comes to current and future referrals."

Consider niches or groups with which you already are associated. Once you make your first sale, you should be able to develop contacts with other people within the group and, over time, create a steady stream of referrals.

• **Strategic Partner Referral Network:** In addition to potential customers, your referral network should include strategic business partners with whom you have regular contact, typically other professionals who are in a position to exchange referrals. They may include attorneys, CPAs, financial planners, business managers, and mortgage lenders. Make sure these valuable contacts are aware of your interest in receiving their referrals. It's also important that they know about any of your specialty areas or points of distinction, so they can make the strongest potential referral. There is a huge difference between this referral: "You really want to talk about that purchase with *him* because he is an expert and the absolute best in his field," and this one: "Give him a call and he should be able to take care of you."

Sharing referrals is a key to success with strategic business partners; it can't be a one-way process. Don't be stingy. If you do not reciprocate, your associates will eventually get tired of recommending people to you. One of my most effective business-building strategies as a new originator was to bring new prospects to realtors without asking for anything in return. I would meet with a real estate agent with whom I hadn't previously worked and mention that I had someone who was looking for a home, and then referred them to that agent. This practice was somewhat unusual at the time and the agents responded well by eventually referring numerous people to me.

Partner Referrals

Meet with your primary strategic partners – these are professionals, not your usual customers – with whom you have regular contact, such as attorneys, CPAs, business managers and financial planners. Explain that you think there is an opportunity to grow each other's businesses by sharing referrals. Ask them if there are any restrictions, such as prospects with whom they prefer not to work. Develop an informal arrangement (a more formal agreement may limit you from receiving other referrals) by which you agree to refer clients who have a need for each other's products or services.

In addition to providing direct referrals, there are other ways to support strategic referral partners so they will be inclined to share with you. This could involve assisting them with a community fundraising program, offering advice on a marketing campaign, or just demonstrating your loyalty as a professional.

• **Unusual Sources:** We typically think of receiving referrals from those customers who rave about our service and can't wait to tell their friends and work associates about us. However, it is also possible to receive referrals from more unlikely sources, such as someone you previously weren't able to help. "I have found that you can get referrals from someone you have to turn down, who wasn't able to get a loan from you," said one of my colleagues. "If you treat someone you have to turn down correctly, giving them respect and sound advice on where they can go to get financing, they can become a great referral source. I think many people think of a turndown as just that, and the end of the relationship. That is just not true; I have people I wasn't able to arrange a loan for who continue to send me referrals."

You may not offer the insurance policy, computer, camera, HDTV, or other product that a prospect wants, but if you make a positive impression and demonstrate your interest in being helpful, he may be motivated to refer you to others.

In addition, your competitors can be good referral sources. If you offer a specific product or service that a competitor doesn't, wouldn't you rather have them refer that business to you? If you aren't able to provide a specific product, you should feel comfortable recommending someone to another salesperson you feel can be trusted to handle the sale without "stealing" your regular customer. Most customers recognize that this sort of cross-referral serves their best interests, and they will appreciate it.

To make the competitive referral networking effective, you need to be familiar enough with the competing salesperson to know they are professional, will provide excellent service, and aren't interested in diverting the customer's future purchases. If you have a solid relationship with your customer, you should not be overly concerned that they will leave you.

Don't Take Customers for Granted

As with any sales relationship, it is vital that you avoid irritating customers and others by ignoring or otherwise disappointing their referrals. I encountered this potential problem first-hand when a long-time client referred someone to me whose property had appraisal issues that I knew were going to create a significant challenge for us in obtaining his loan. When the transaction didn't work out for the new prospect, my customer sent me a note indicating his displeasure that I had not been able to help his friend. Obviously, if I had ignored this note or appeared defensive, I would have risked losing future referrals. Instead, I followed-up quickly and addressed the issue positively, after which my client understood and has continued sending me customers.

There are other times when a referral may not work out. For instance, I have had referred prospects call me and say that they have already talked to several other loan originators, but if I can provide the lowest rate they will probably go with me. Because I am not interested in competing for loan shoppers, I explain that they would probably be better off continuing to deal with the other originator who had made the big promises. I then call my customer to explain that while I appreciate his referral, I wasn't the appropriate person to assist his friend. Again, I make a point to explain the situation to my referral sources and they usually understand.

Always remember that an unhappy referral can sour the relationship with your original customer. A once never-ending supply of referrals can dry up quickly, simply because you didn't take the time to satisfy a frustrated prospect. The key is to put out fires immediately. If there's a problem, answer it quickly so that your referral partner is satisfied.

Just think how much extra business you would have today if you had started a proactive referral program, or expanded your existing one, a few years ago. It doesn't take a great deal of effort. You already have a database of satisfied customers, just waiting to hand you their referrals.

But don't forget you also have to ask for the business.

Chapter Thirteen
Requesting Referrals:
You Don't Ask, You Won't Receive

It isn't sufficient just to want – you've got to ask yourself what you are going to do to get the things you want.
- Franklin D. Roosevelt

You are most likely excited about the potential of receiving a huge number of referrals that you'll get, simply because you do a good job.

However, think of all the other valuable referrals you may not be receiving today for one reason: you haven't asked for them.

Asking for referrals is really a basic, straightforward strategy. All you have to do is remind satisfied customers you would appreciate them recommending you to their friends, family members, and others. If you have done a good job with the customer's transaction – made a good impression and had a trouble-free sale – they should want to recommend you.

Yet, some salespeople hesitate to ask because they don't want to seem needy or pushy. They may feel that their products and exceptional service should be enough to prompt a customer to share referrals, and in many cases, that is sufficient.

The bottom line is that if you do not ask, you won't receive. While I am sufficiently busy with existing business from my past customers and their referrals, I continue to encourage everyone to recommend me to their friends, neighbors, and others. Is any salesperson really too busy to accept an enthusiastic referral? I doubt it.

How and When to Ask

Asking for referrals is an ongoing process. Depending on your profession, you can ask for a referral the first time you meet a prospect, at any point during the transaction, when the sale is completed, or whenever else you deem it to be appropriate. There is no set schedule.

Customers are usually most receptive to a referral request at the completion of the initial transaction, when they are excited about the purchase and ready to tell other people about their positive experience. For example, during a loan closing, most borrowers are ecstatic that the wait is over and that they will soon move into their dream home. There are usually happy real estate agents and attorneys in the room as well, making this a particularly referral-rich environment. All salespeople have similar opportunities.

Referral Timeline

Create a formal referral system that includes a checklist to help you remember to ask for referrals during your initial conversation with customers, at the conclusion of a sale, and in follow-up communications. Be consistent – ask at the same times with every customer. If necessary, prepare a script that you can use in telephone conversations. Make notations on the checklist every time you ask.

At the other end of the spectrum, I have had many customers begin our very first conversation with "If you do a good job for me, I know several other people who will be interested in talking with you." Of course, I am going to serve them well anyway, but you can bet that I subsequently remind them, "Don't forget to mention me to those three people you talked about earlier."

One of the most basic and effective referral requests is: "I'm glad you're happy with the product. Please let me know if you are aware of a family member, work associate, or friend for whom I can offer the same level of service that I have tried to provide for you...." You are emphasizing that you will take good care of the customer's friend or relative, and that should be enough to inspire them to recommend you. People usually respond positively when you phrase the request as if you're doing something to help others. You may also be appealing to their egos, implying that they have access to an extensive Rolodex of referral sources.

I often give customers extra encouragement during our conversations. For instance, I will say something like, "I'm glad I was able to help you achieve your home ownership goals, and I hope you share that experience with neighbors and friends. You know, by the end of their own transactions, the majority of my customers have already referred several people to me. So please feel free to let me know about anyone could benefit from my service."

Sales professionals who deal with extended transactions, such as arranging insurance policies, financial plans or mortgage loans, will usually have many good chances to remind customers that they appreciate referrals.

Creative Asking

Look for creative ways to ask for referrals. For example, you could wear a button that says, "Ask Me How I Can Help Your Family & Friends." When a customer or prospect tells you to explain, simply respond "I can provide them with the same great service that hopefully you agree I provided for you (or "That I am about to provide…"). I will take good care of them." This not only prompts customers to encourage their family and friends to purchase from you, it also engages them in a conversation about how you were able to assist them.

In addition to asking during your regular conversations with customers, you will find other ways to highlight your interest in referrals. For instance, add a line to your business card, as an email tag line, Facebook page or website announcement: "I thrive on referrals," "Your referrals are important to me," or "I welcome the opportunity to help your friends, family, and work colleagues." You can also highlight specific examples of how your product or service has helped customers meet their needs. Include these case history testimonials in a newsletter, website article or other promotional material.

Some situations don't offer as many opportunities to request referrals. For example, it may be more challenging to find appropriate times to ask for referrals in a retail environment. However, it should not be difficult to tell a customer who has just purchased a new TV, computer, or sofa, "Don't forget to tell your family and friends about us. And, be sure to suggest that they ask for me."

Avoid Overaggressive Approach

You have to be careful not to push too hard when asking for referrals. I know of some loan originators and other salespeople who give their customers a form to complete before the transaction is complete. The salesperson points to the five blank spaces, expecting the customer to fill in the names right then. This may work fine with those of your customers who are so enthusiastic at their purchase that they eagerly suggest names of potential customers. Others may consider it too aggressive, so you would need to use this strategy carefully.

I have also witnessed an even more demanding referral request. I remember a salesperson who tried to gain my sympathy about his recent sales slump. He said that he was in jeopardy of losing his job but that my purchase would make him feel more secure, and if I could recommend at least two additional prospects, he would be even more confident. It was a desperate way of asking for referrals, and you can be sure that I didn't add him to my short list of sales reps to call or recommend.

Acknowledging Referrals

Salespeople often feel they have to reward their referral sources with a gift: flowers, a bottle of wine, or something more. Of course, you need to confirm that gift-giving is allowed in your industry. In mortgage lending and probably other professions, it is illegal to provide "something of value" in exchange for referrals. Therefore, you are not able to send a gift card, book, or other item as a thank you for recommending customers.

Plus, you need to consider if it's really necessary. I have found a thank you card is enough. Customers normally feel that you taking care of their friend or relative with excellent service is sufficient acknowledgement of their generosity. I frequently refer customers to a bankruptcy attorney, who sends me a thank-you note along with two business cards. I always call and personally thank people whenever they have referred customers to me. It doesn't take much to show your appreciation.

Monitoring Referrals

It is essential that you know the number of referrals customers and others provide over a period of time so that you can monitor the effectiveness of various referral partners. Maintaining and analyzing the information can help you spot trends, such as an overall decrease in referrals, or a rise in referrals from specific categories. If you discover that a long-time business associate begins to refer people to a competitor, you can discuss the issue with your contact.

Having easy access to this information also gives you an advantage when talking with customers. When a past customer calls, I can make a comment about his recent referrals during our conversation: "Thanks for referring me to Mr. Jones last month. I know I'll be able to help him. Now, how can I assist you today?"

It is easy to get so busy that you forget to ask for referrals. Or you just assume that satisfied customers will remember and mention your name to their friends and work associates. Don't risk losing an on-going source of business. Take a few minutes to ask, and you will receive.

Chapter Fourteen

Smart Marketing: Make It Creative,
Simple and Effective

The aim of marketing is to know and understand the customer so well the product or service fits him and sells itself. - Peter Drucker

Just imagine wearing a "sandwich board" sign over your head to advertise a new product or service. It's hard to believe, but that was one of the popular marketing techniques some salespeople used long ago to entice their customers into buying.

My own marketing has evolved greatly, from my first experience as a "black market" salesman in Ukraine, to my time as an assistant manager at a McDonald's restaurant, to my start in the mortgage-lending industry.

I refined my marketing expertise significantly when I became a loan originator, testing everything from cold calling, to small space newspaper ads, to T-shirts that announced the opening of Gold Star Mortgage.

While I now have access to a much larger marketing budget than I had as a novice salesman, there are some essential marketing principles that haven't changed. All salespeople, and certainly those aspiring

to be superstars, must establish some type of marketing campaign to remain competitive, and it is important to put your own individual stamp on traditional marketing strategies. Remember, though, it is better to be a "smart" marketer than a flashy one. The main elements of a comprehensive marketing campaign include tactics I've highlighted in earlier chapters, such as referral networking and customer-for-life strategies.

Smart Marketing

At some point in your sales career you have probably encountered The 5 Ps of Marketing—Product, Price, Physical Distribution, Promotion and People (customer service). Most salespeople only have direct control over the last two Ps.

Analyze Past Marketing Efforts

If you have not done so recently, take time to do a simple evaluation of your past marketing work. List everything you (not the company) have done in the last two years, from distributing fliers, to advertising, to website announcements. Note the results for each, whether or not you have received calls, inquiries, or sales following a specific strategy. If you haven't tracked results, start doing so now. At the very least, ask new customers "How did you hear about me?"

The most important aspect of promotion is following smart marketing guidelines, which include:

• Being organized, having a plan.

• Producing results.

• Using simple/effective strategies that "won't break the bank."

• Being creative, an out-of-the-box thinker when appropriate.

• Maintaining consistency.

Smart marketing involves "trial and error," practice, and ongoing adjustments. I consider myself a relatively wise marketer now, but it was not an overnight process. I never wore a sandwich sign, but did hand out my share of doughnuts.

Develop a Plan

Just as you need an overall plan that establishes your sales projections, key strategies and overall operational directions, you need a separate marketing plan. Even if your marketing is still on a basic level, it should be carefully organized.

Consider the full range of available marketing strategies, including direct mail, advertising, social media, special events, and community involvement activities. Organize them into priorities based on how well they communicate your message, if they reach the intended audiences, whether they fit your budget, and other factors. Determine a reasonable schedule for implementing the appropriate strategies.

Your marketing plan must have distinctive goals and objectives, so you can reach your audience and generate the desired results. For example, you need to determine whether you are seeking brand awareness, so that people begin to recognize you as the most knowledgeable, experienced salesperson in your market, or you are trying to achieve more immediate sales results. My early marketing techniques were primarily aimed at generating a quick response. My emails, letters and phone calls were all based on one simple objective: I wanted to persuade people to ask me to handle their refinance or purchase loans. My current efforts are focused on longer-range branding objectives.

To establish your own marketing presence, you must have a good understanding of how others in your area promote themselves. Are there some creative or successful strategies that other salespeople have implemented? Take time to analyze a newspaper advertisement, business Facebook page, or brochure. Ask customers and prospects what attracts them to other salespeople. Perhaps they respond best to newsletters, email announcements or websites. If appropriate, adapt a few of your competitor's strategies to fit your own style.

Whether you are seeking long-term market awareness or a more immediate return, it's essential that you carefully measure results, which is a major challenge for all salespeople. Of course, your criteria for success may vary. For example, you may determine that a worthwhile outcome of a specific marketing campaign is receiving 50 calls or prospect visits – many of which could be future customers – but only five initial sales.

There are some easy ways to measure short- and long-term results, such as asking prospects how they heard about you, and calculating the number of responses generated from a specific strategy.

Make It Simple

Many salespeople ignore some of the most basic marketing techniques. You don't need a large budget to develop an effective campaign.

Street Marketing – The early salesmen who "peddled" vacuum cleaners and encyclopedia sets followed one of the most basic marketing strategies: door-to-door sales. In a sense, that is also how I got started, meeting prospects at realtor, builder, attorney, CPA and other offices. I spent many days calling on prospects, which enabled me to establish long-term business relationships that otherwise would have taken longer to make.

Even salespeople "confined" to a retail store could consider visiting potential customers. You could be the first to suggest the idea to your sales manager, who might then let you test it on a few nearby companies. This could also offer an opportunity to negotiate for an appropriate commission adjustment.

Street marketing is a great way to selectively expand your customer base in key areas. Even those of you who already are on your way to becoming a superstar should consider this as an ideal opportunity to get up close with prospects.

Daily Contacts – Another under-utilized marketing technique involves making a specific number of contacts each day. For example, you set a goal of completing a certain number of calls or emails to introduce yourself, your products or services, and your interest in assisting potential customers.

Start by calling 10 people every day and let them know you are always available to help them. My fashion advisor, a top clothing salesman, often calls people primarily on a personal basis, without mentioning a clothing sale or other promotion. He'll call just to say hello, more as a friend than a salesman. When they ask what's new in the store, he'll tell them and suggest they stop by. It's a soft and cheap marketing technique.

He also takes the time to write letters to prospects and customers and often includes an article that may be of interest. For example, if he reads an article in the paper about someone he'd like to have as a customer, he will mail a copy with a note, such as "Looks like you're doing well." It lets the customer know he's thinking about them.

Publicity – Sometimes called "free advertising," publicity does require an investment of time, but is otherwise one of the most cost-effective marketing activities available.

Your corporate public relations director may have control over most of the product announcements, but there is another effective tool, the "how to" column or blog. You can suggest to the local newspaper business editor that you will provide a regular column on topics relevant to your field, such as "How to Shop for a Laptop," or "The 10 Secrets to Buying a Car."

In addition, you can gradually build your reputation among business editors as the go-to person to contact when they need background information or a quote for an article. During the last 10 years, I have contributed numerous articles and been quoted by various media outlets, which has helped enhance my reputation as an expert in my field. I also know many other excellent salespeople who have used publicity to expand their overall name recognition and sales volume.

Fliers – Most salespeople have used flier marketing at one time or another, usually to announce a sale or new service. I frequently created fliers highlighting current interest rates along with my emphasis on customer service, and handed them out at the offices of realtors and builders.

One interesting application for fliers is to incorporate an offer of a free guide. For example, as an incentive for prospects to call or email you for information, you can provide them with a flier-guide that features "Answers to the Top House Repair Challenges," or "New Car Selection," or "Buying a New Wardrobe," or whatever may be applicable to your field. These brief guides are simple to develop, and are usually appreciated by prospects who are looking for helpful information.

Advertise – Advertising can be expensive, but there may be a few viable options you haven't considered. For example, have you thought about placing an ad in your church bulletin, high school athletic program, or college alumni directory? These publications are aimed at very select audiences and you should certainly be able to afford a small ad in one or more of them. You can also advertise your product or service in such online forums as Craigslist, often at no cost. One of my first marketing techniques was running a small ad in the local shopper, with great results.

Creative and Consistent

The best marketing programs combine tested and proven strategies with more creative or innovative elements. I have developed a basic approach that applies to both individual and corporate marketing programs. Eighty percent of my marketing focuses on "proven" techniques which have generated results, such as direct mailers and advertising. I aim the remaining 20 percent at those newer, more outside-the-box strategies I believe are worth testing, which have included everything from inserting fliers in pizza boxes for delivery to CPA offices, to a million dollar giveaway promotion with the Detroit Red Wings.

Sometimes, unavoidable circumstances may force you to be extra creative in your marketing efforts. A good example of that was when designer Kenneth Cole wanted to showcase his new line of shoes during fashion week at the Hilton Hotel in New York. Because he couldn't afford to rent a showroom to exhibit his shoes, Cole decided a unique option would be to sell them on the street. However, he learned that the only companies that could get street permits were utility and movie companies. So he changed his letterhead to Kenneth Cole Productions and went to city hall to apply for a permit to film "The Birth of a Shoe Company." They had a fully-furnished 40-foot trailer, stage lights, director, and models as actresses. He definitely attracted attention and sold 40,000 pairs of shoes in less than three days.

Budget

Be sure to develop your own marketing budget. If you don't have the funds necessary to achieve your marketing goals right now, you should be setting money aside. If company restrictions prevent you from conducting individual marketing campaigns, you may want to establish a fund for a time when you will have more flexibility, which may be at a different company.

The 80/20 formula is one I have developed over time; you have to consider what is most effective for your situation. You've also got to keep up with the marketing trends. A specific concept that was effective a few years ago might not be appropriate for today.

Remember that your marketing does not have to be a totally new concept; there really aren't any completely new ideas. However, it may often be new to your market or something your customers have not previously seen.

Obviously, your results will also be greater if you have a consistent marketing presence. People often cut marketing expenditures during slower periods. Most experts will tell you this is precisely the wrong time to stop. By continuing to market at some level, you will avoid losing the momentum you have already developed, and also be able to take advantage of business left behind by competitors who reduce their marketing efforts.

It is generally better to establish a more modest marketing campaign that you will be able to execute, rather than a more complex or expensive program that you'll have to cut back because of budget or other limitations. You have to be patient, allowing time for your strategies to develop and either show signs of success, or failure, in which case you'll discard the failures for more effective ones.

You may not be ready for prime time, showcasing your photo and contact information on expensive billboards or TV ads, but there is nothing to stop you from handing out a flier at the local parade, fair, or pancake breakfast.

Chapter Fifteen

Social Media: Everyone Needs Friends

It's a dialogue, not a monologue, and some people don't understand that. Social media is more like a telephone than a television. - Amy Jo Martin

I n theory, it is possible to be a successful salesperson without having a presence on the World Wide Web. In reality, you would be missing out on a great deal of business.

Just in case you are one of the few who hasn't yet realized it, a social media platform is a great way to create relationships that can lead to sales. You are connecting with people who could be interested in your product or service, en masse.

Though younger salespeople came of age tethered to smart phones and laptops and are accustomed to using innovative social media techniques, we have all had to adapt to this major force affecting our business and personal lives. The new generation of salespeople realize that an ever-increasing number of consumers rely on the Internet for product information and make decisions based on their online research. They know that social media is an essential path to generating short- and long-term business, and supercharging their networking efforts.

Traditional communication vehicles have become less popular than the more time efficient social media tactics. For instance, one study confirmed that while on vacation, 60 percent of people sent text messages to family and friends, but only 16 percent mailed postcards. This simple stat exemplifies our tightening schedules and shrinking attention spans. We consume and provide information on our own schedules and an online presence allows a salesperson to be prepared to address potential customers 24/7. Certainly that is just one small example, but it does highlight the ever-increasing impact that social media has on both our personal and business lives.

While many companies use their social media assets as distribution channels for marketing material, the dissemination of information is only a fraction of what social media can do. A carefully selected platform can be a well-honed tool for you to have a conversation with your colleagues, customers, competitors, etc.

Getting customers' attention is increasingly difficult. Many emails are marked as spam before they even hit your prospect's inbox, and the sheer volume of those that manage to get through makes standing out from the crowd extremely difficult. Of the few emails your prospect does open, click-through rates (CTRs) are declining.

Nonetheless, Facebook, Twitter, and LinkedIn are large networks seen by many as standard, and while some prospects may not notice that you are online, a customer will certainly notice if you are not.

Selecting a platform which suits your business is important. When developing a social media strategy, limit yourself to a handful of platforms, at most. Social media can be influential in driving sales, customer care, and business and personal reputation management. But spreading yourself thinly across too many platforms can actually prevent you from genuinely and meaningfully engaging with your prospects. Make sure you understand the social-psychological demographic of your audience for a given social media platform, to make sure it suits your business.

Managing a social media channel is certainly an opportunity, but it is also a task that requires an investment of your time. As with any professional goal, you need to determine how you will measure success and what the Key Performance Indicators (KPI) will be. Once you identify the KPIs, then you can select one or more social media platforms to leverage for that opportunity. Likewise, an analysis of your target demographic—determining which social media networks they use most—will let you determine which platforms will best help you reach your objectives.

As noted, there are many social media channels available to a salesperson, but the following three have emerged in recent history as frontrunners in the number of active users and user engagement.

LinkedIn

LinkedIn is certainly the most cost-effective networking and business-building strategy available, one that more salespeople should be incorporating into their ongoing marketing campaign. It is a free platform for creating a substantial presence with other professionals and networking. The key to LinkedIn success is to be an active participant. After creating a complete profile, you should share helpful information with your "Connections" to further identify yourself as a "thought leader." This can include regular notices highlighting a survey, report, trend or other information that is useful, relevant, and stimulating to your audience. Take care to reference only credible sources, as each posting speaks to your business acumen. Here are a few examples:

- How to Navigate a Changing Health Care Environment.
- Can Renting Cure the Housing Market Blues?
- U.S. Employment Increased in July.
- 8 Tips for Furniture Shopping in Thrift Stores.

Show Your Expertise

Once you have added your complete LinkedIn profile, evaluate the type of "news" you can share with your Connections. For example, look for studies and other value-add items relating to your specific industry, general business tips, and motivational messages. You can also join and contribute to "Groups" that deal with topics of interest to you and your customers. Be mindful of the fact that some groups may not be worth your time. Before joining, read recent posts to decide if the writers are people with whom you will want to interact.

Be wary of excessive posting or self promotion, or your audience may tune you out. Keep the proper

balance of tips and other helpful information that he-
maintains your image as the expert, along with subtle
product or service messages.

Facebook

Facebook has an even greater potential audience
than LinkedIn, with an estimated one-billion-plus
users, even though many consider it to be primarily
a social news exchange. For some it's like being at a
cocktail party where guests ramble on and on about
themselves, their hobbies, children, pets, and everything else, without taking a real interest in you.

People do get bored hearing about the various personal updates. You should always strive for
a balance, sharing information that appeals to you,
whether that is sports, fashion, or business, while also
making an effort to take an interest in your Friends.
You can pose questions, which will further help attract people to your page. Remember that Facebook
offers you a chance to show your personal side as well
as your business expertise. You're giving people another opportunity to relate to you, which can evolve
into a business relationship.

If you're going to include information about your
products and services on your personal Facebook
page, you might consider including a special promotion or discount every so often.

Generally, it's a good idea to have a separate business page that won't attract those who are more con-

cerned with exchanging recipes, vacation plans, and children's photos. You can post helpful hints related to your service or product. Include articles you wrote or found, as well as things your target market might find interesting even if they aren't directly related to what you're selling.

I developed a separate professional page to share some of the ideas from *The ABC of Sales* and my various presentations, which I believe further helps to position me as an industry leader. I don't use this page to do any direct marketing, such as emphasizing mortgage products or interest rates.

You need to pay attention and respond to your Facebook friends' status updates, which may involve business-related questions. For example, you may notice that one of your friends (or their friends) is asking questions about obtaining insurance, ideas on computer applications, or some other subject related to your product or service. It is critical that you take advantage of these often subtle queries.

Of course, you want to be sure to promote your LinkedIn and Facebook presence. For example, send emails inviting your clients and referral partners to become one of your Connections or Friends. You can also include the Facebook icon link in your email signature. Then, anyone who receives an email from you can just click on that link and it takes them to your Facebook page.

Twitter

Many salespeople probably find it challenging to condense their messages into 140 characters. It does take practice. Similar to LinkedIn messages, you want your tweets to be interesting and of real value. Ideal subjects might include a survey or economic report that may impact their business, a consumer-buying trend, or a business-building tip. Twitter messages can have real impact when a customer or prospect receives them during a free moment on the road, or even while in a meeting.

Get Organized:

Plan ahead when considering your future tweets. Practice converting your longer copy into the 140 character messages. Try to outline a series of future topics, so that you can ensure your tweets will be of interest and well received. Develop a regular schedule, tweeting once a day, weekly or at whatever interval you can establish.

You can develop a Twitter audience by emailing an example of a typical tweet to your regular database or another group, ideally enticing them to sign up to receive future messages. Twitter makes it relatively easy to find people with common interests by searching for key words. For example, you can search for anyone who is tweeting about cars, furniture or a house and reach out to them if that's what you're selling.

If you're away from your computer, you can easily send tweets from your smart phone, using one of the specially designed applications. This will help minimize any interruptions to your regular work schedule.

If you have not yet started a social media campaign, you can ease into it. Look at what other salespeople in your office or your competitors are doing. Take time to get organized and set your goals, but don't wait too long. It takes time for any social media strategy to build momentum and you want to start meeting new Friends and Connections as soon as possible.

Social media, like all other technology applications, are changing at a rapid pace and will continue to evolve. During the next decade, LinkedIn, Facebook and Twitter will undoubtedly undergo significant enhancements – or they may be completely replaced by new social media developments. Staying agile in the face of this changing technological landscape may seem daunting, but is absolutely manageable if you dedicate a couple of hours a month to reading about advancements.

Chapter Sixteen
Ongoing Education: Get Smarter Faster

Formal education will make you a living; self-education will make you a fortune. - Jim Rohn

I don't know everything. I'll bet you don't either.

While I consider myself very knowledgeable about the mortgage lending industry, sales, and other areas, I realize there is always more to learn. I remember when I was a new salesperson and someone told me, "As soon as you think you know everything in this business, you are set to fail..." At that moment, I promised myself that I would never stop my professional education.

We are all acquainted with more than one "know-it-all." These are people who think they have completely mastered their profession, who believe that there is nothing else for them to learn.

Being recognized as "the expert" means that you

must strive to be more knowledgeable than your competitors. Your credibility will suffer if the people with whom you do business ever get the idea you aren't familiar with your products, industry trends, or the basic sales process.

The best salespeople never stop learning. They take advantage of all available resources, knowing that by doing so they will not only be in a better position to help their customers, but will also ensure their own superstar status.

Assessing Your Sales IQ

Even the most successful salespeople have gaps in their education, and should periodically do a self-assessment. For example, ask yourself if you are sufficiently well versed in:

• **Your company's products and services.** This seems obvious, but you must have a deep understanding of more than just the highlights of your products and services. For example, you should be able to compare your products with the competition's selection.

• **Industry trends.** Having an understanding of the industry's potential changes and the demographic shifts within your main customer base will let you adapt your sales strategies to just about anything that might happen.

Develop An Agenda

Once you determine what is lacking in your sales education, develop a training agenda, including books to read and audio programs to review. Include a timeline to complete your assignments. Study industry publications and online forums that offer advanced ideas and information. Attend seminars and conferences specific to your field. As you gain expertise in specific areas, you can even "switch sides" and participate at these conferences. Sometimes teaching is the best way to expand your knowledge.

• **Technology.** Many veteran salespeople have a hard time adjusting to the rapid pace of technological advances. You don't have to be a tech expert, but you should have a working knowledge of subjects like database management, website maintenance, Internet research and Facebook marketing. If nothing else, you need to be able to communicate with the tech geeks you will need to hire.

• **Marketing strategies.** We've already discussed this in detail. The message is that the more you know about marketing yourself, the greater long-term recognition you can generate.

• **People skills.** Perhaps it's time to brush up on your interpersonal skills, how you interact with customers and others.

You must be a tough self-critic, objectively evaluating the areas that require improvement. If you have doubts about specific areas, outline the steps that will help make a difference.

Early in my sales career, I was having difficulty, not able to succeed at the level I wanted. One evening, I made a list of the areas that were lacking in my sales education. I concluded that the most glaring omission in my previous training was the ability to actually close the sale. I didn't have a sufficient understanding of the operational side of the business. I outlined the steps necessary to overcome this deficiency, which included observing other successful salespeople, further reading of industry publications, and of course, more on-the-job exercises. This personal lesson plan helped me turn the corner and eventually become very successful.

Take Advantage of Available Resources

During the last decade there has been an increase in the number of well written, informative sales books. Such authors as Brian Tracy and Harvey Mackay have contributed some great insights on sales techniques, human interaction, and other subjects. I frequently visit Amazon.com and our area's bookstores, always searching for something new to read that might make me a little smarter.

You should also bookmark your favorite websites so you can refer to them on a daily basis. Stay abreast of the latest developments in your industry, the market, and general economy. I typically spend a half-hour each morning and afternoon reviewing the Merrill Lynch Report, Bloomberg, and CNBC. I also listen to Bloomberg Radio while driving to and from work.

Make sure you take advantage of company training as well. Sales-related training has significantly improved during the last few years, doing away with the old idea of "do-it-yourself" instruction. This does not mean there isn't room for improvement in these efforts, but an increasing number of companies do offer their sales staff and other personnel valuable educational opportunities.

Your company may have a training room stocked with books, CDs, and other resource material. If your management hasn't had the foresight to develop such a training resource area, now might be a good time to suggest that it does so. At Gold Star, we encourage our staff to continue learning and share books and CDs on a variety of topics.

You should definitely take advantage of the resources offered by your industry associations and related groups. This includes visiting association websites, reading organization publications, and attending industry conferences. If your company budget does not include travel expenses for out-of-state programs, cover the cost yourself or attend similar local programs.

Online Education

There are numerous sales-related websites that feature helpful information on a variety of topics. Of course, some are part of an online university's curriculum and will require a fee. However, others are free and include articles, book reviews, and related resources that should be useful. Do an Internet search or ask colleagues to suggest their favorites.

Coaches Can Be Great Teachers

Coaches play an increasingly important role in helping salespeople reach a greater level of success. I consider coaching to be an extension of the "never stop learning" concept.

Salespeople who work with coaches often emphasize that doing so helps them to be more accountable. The salesperson establishes specific goals, and the coach "keeps their feet to the fire," ensuring that they stick to a timetable for accomplishing the agreed-to tasks.

A coach serves as a cheerleader as well as a supportive taskmaster. While many sales managers will insist this is their role, I think a coach can offer a more objective viewpoint to aid the salesperson. Coaches can help you become smarter with:

• **Setting appropriate goals.** Salespeople and other professionals often have trouble setting timely and achievable goals. For instance, they may set the production bar too low and thus "settle" for something less than their best. Or in some cases, they set an exceptionally high goal that is virtually impossible to reach. I know that in my early days as a salesman, I probably set extra-lofty goals that were hard to achieve without working extremely long hours. A coach would most likely have advised me to adjust these sales targets, and hopefully I would not have been too stubborn to pay attention.

• **Establishing and Managing Priorities.** Even the most successful salespeople often find it a challenge to make time to accomplish their primary goals, continually increase sales and, of course, maintain a balance between their work and personal lives. A coach can serve as a monitor, working with you to help adjust plans and schedules so you are better able to focus on the most essential priorities.

Throughout my sales career, I have had a number of supervisors, advisors, and confidants I could trust to offer me encouragement, objective advice, and even a firm push. However, none were professionally-trained coaches, and I'm sure I would have benefitted greatly from having one – especially during the first few years I was striving to become a high-volume producer. I pushed myself hard enough that I didn't need anyone to hold me accountable for my monthly or annual sales goals, or to establish the necessary work ethic. However, a good coach could have been helpful in organizing my priorities in other areas.

Check Your Priorities

Evaluate your primary sales activity over the last two weeks and note if you have let any critical tasks slide into the "do later" category. If this happens often, it could be an indication you need a coach to keep you on track to meet your goals.

My brother Alex, one of the nation's top real estate agents, credits his coach with helping him attain even greater sales success. I know many other salespeople who also have benefitted from working with a coach. While some are newer salespeople who want to establish good habits from the beginning of their careers, I have also talked to a number of top producers who have emphasized the advantage of working with a coach even when they are at the peak of their profession. They stress that as their production increases and marketing and sales activities require more of their time, a coach keeps them focused on their priority goals.

Obviously, you want to take advantage of any coaching program your company offers. In addition, talk to other salespeople about their coaching experiences and determine whether or not it makes sense for you.

Hiring a coach is an option. However, continuing to learn by studying about the economy, your industry, and everything else that will make you more effective is an absolute necessity. Stop learning and you will soon become just an average salesperson, falling behind competitors who have remained current as the experts in their fields.

15 Suggestions for Sales Managers

Sell with your salespeople. It's easy to forget what it is like to actually sell. Go on a few outside sales calls with them so that you have a current perspective on what "street selling" is like.

Raise the bar realistically. Just as salespeople should push themselves, so should you give them higher targets to reach. Make sure that they are both aggressive and achievable.

Support them with resources. Find the resources that will help the sales team be more productive. If necessary, expand your budget. If this is not possible, rather than say "Of course, we can't pay for that," give them ideas on how they can do something positive on their own.

Establish a mentor program. Give newer salespeople a chance to learn from the more experienced ones.

Develop and demand a positive work experience. Successful and positive people generally tend to influence others with a similar attitude. Conversely, if you have salespeople complaining about the economy, their sales slump, and other challenges, they tend to create a negative atmosphere. You may even need to eliminate bad performers; "prune" the team.

Have an open door policy. Encourage everyone to stop by your office to discuss sales strategies and concerns.

Motivate the most improved. A part of your incentive campaign should reward the most improved salespeople.

Create or enhance your training program. If you don't have a library of sales books, CDs and industry publications, start one now. If possible, invite speakers to your monthly meeting and encourage salespeople to attend seminars and other programs.

Watch for burnout. It is great to see your salespeople working overtime to produce results, but don't let them burn out. Watch for signs of fatigue and help them maintain a proactive and healthy work ethic.

Review the fundamentals. Make sure that all salespeople have the same basic understanding of the sales process, from the first conversation to the close. Hold a workshop to correct any misconceptions.

Create a plan with them. Help your team members develop individual long-term growth plans that include an evaluation of strengths and weaknesses, along with action steps to improvement.

Don't approach every employee the same way. What may motivate one could potentially impede another. Identify what makes each of your salespeople "tick" and capitalize on that.

Reward multiple factors, not just production. In addition to sales volume, be sure to place an equal emphasis on teamwork and loyalty. This will pay great dividends.

Provide coaching advice early. You want to address performance-related challenges as soon as possible. Monitor performance closely so that you can help convert those learning-curve blunders into newly polished skills.

Maintain a winning attitude. You want salespeople who are confident and enthusiastic about the future. Look for ways to instill a "can do" attitude. This can also be a benefit in recruiting new talent, when others see your staff and want to be part of the team.

Chapter Seventeen

Adapting to Change: Old Dogs and Most Salespeople Can Learn New Tricks

There are two primary choices in life: to accept conditions as they exist or accept the responsibility for changing them. - Denis Waitley

There have been a few occasions when I have asked myself a very serious question, which fortunately I have not yet had to address:

If I wasn't originating mortgages, what else could I sell?

That is actually a question I considered during the infamous mortgage meltdown of 2007-09. When the mortgage lending industry was in a tailspin, and so many loan originators were worried about their futures, I had to wonder about my own. I had to remain positive around our employees, and strongly believed that our company would survive. But I did have to at least consider the possibility that I would need to move into a different industry.

This is something all salespeople need to consider. If you aren't flexible – able and willing to make both minor and major adjustments in your sales career – you could be out of a job.

Refining and Reinventing

There are many situations in which salespeople have to switch gears, to reinvent themselves in order to stay competitive, or even to remain in business. For example, one of the most common mid-course corrections involves re-evaluating your existing customer base. I have experienced this on several occasions. For example, early in my career a large percentage of my customers were Russian immigrants. I eventually realized the need to expand, and began working with professional athletes and other groups.

If your product or service appeals to an especially narrow audience you may be in jeopardy of reaching a plateau from which it becomes difficult to expand your production. You may find that you are unable to grow your business without developing additional prospect sources. If so, you need to continue exploring other types of prospects who may have an interest in and need for your product.

There are other situations that may require you to adjust your long-term strategy. For example, if changing demographics indicate customers' preferences for different products or services, you may have to modify your own offerings. The real challenge is to develop a Plan B that will help you adjust to a significantly changing sales environment.

For example, what if your company revamped its operational focus and dropped a product line that you have handled exclusively? Would you be able to adapt quickly and transfer into a new department? Or would it be better for you to relocate to a different firm that carried the products with which you are most familiar?

A good Plan B should include an evaluation of:

• **Your current skill set.**

• **Your past experience,** including work in different professions.

• **Other local companies** that offer products or services with which you have the most experience.

Obviously the most crucial element of a full Plan
B is to consider the possibility of a major change in
your industry that could require you to sell a completely new product or service.

Update Your Profile

Create a Plan B summary of your
potential options. Consider the
other product or service categories
you might be comfortable selling, and
note any special requirements, additional education,
experience, skill transferability, market choices, and
income potential.

If your industry went into a major, ongoing
slump, would you be prepared to make a move to
a different field? If you determined it was no longer financially feasible to sell computers, insurance
policies, or high end cars, what would you do? Some
salespeople are great at selling tangible products, but
they may not be nearly as successful with services,
such as financial planning or insurance. I like to think
I could sell almost anything, but in reality I might
not do as well selling office furniture.

When the financial crisis and mortgage lending
industry meltdown occurred, I did dust off my own
"Plan B" and briefly reviewed the options. Sitting
in my office late one afternoon, I made a few notes

about what I could do if the situation got even more serious and the future of our company was in jeopardy. I reminded myself that I could always shut everything down and work from home. Although extremely confident in my ability as an originator, I knew there were other great sales opportunities and I added a few of those to my plan update. However, I didn't give the Plan B alternative much additional thought. Instead, I put it aside and continued to fine-tune a more important document, my plan to determine how Gold Star would not only survive the financial crisis, but thrive while so many others faced layoffs and eventual closure.

Set Your Timetable

How much time would it take for you to make a transition into a totally new industry? Develop a checklist as a guide for what you would need to do. How long would it take for you to acquire the necessary license or certification (as in real estate and mortgage lending), and meet any additional requirements?

Research Now

You need to do the necessary research in advance so that you could be ready for a major move. The first step is to have a good idea of your company's plans.

Are you secure enough in your current position, and do you have a good sense of the company's future directions? If you lack sufficient "inside" knowledge, try to at least get a general perspective of the company's long-range planning from your peers. What other companies in your field are in the immediate market, and do you have contacts there? You should already be knowledgeable about the competition, but you can obtain the essential details by reading local business publications and by talking with vendors and other key contacts.

In addition, evaluate other potential industries. Which ones seem to offer the most logical transition based on your experience, knowledge and other factors? Assess the skills you would need if you switched to another profession. For instance, if you are techphobic and believe it would be difficult to acquire much technology expertise, you probably want to avoid selling computer hardware.

It would be advantageous to consider industries that are relatively recession-proof and that don't have an abundance of sales superstars in your local area.

Making the Move

If the time comes to implement your Plan B because your sales career path appears to be blocked and you have done all the necessary research and planning, you will probably have few doubts. You'll have a clear idea of the seemingly insurmountable obstacles in your path, and will have selected a way around them.

However, if you are thinking of making a change primarily because you think there will be potentially greater financial rewards, or an even less compelling reason, you really need to do some serious "soul searching." First, consider the possibility that you are simply "chasing windfalls," like the opportunistic mortgage salespeople who rushed to our industry during the boom, just to be flushed out when the hard times came.

Second, think about where you are in your sales career. If you are a few years away from retirement, it may simply not be worth the headache to switch. You have to balance the short- and long-term benefits with what it will take to make the change: retraining, adjusting to a new learning curve, local and company competition, and so on. Once you weigh the factors involved, your decision should be clear.

It is probably easier for some of us, but I think most professional salespeople can reinvent themselves. While it may seem unlikely that you will ever need to use a Plan B, most top producers I know don't take their success or their futures for granted. Their back-up plan is an informal insurance policy. They are always ready for change, as you should be.

Chapter Eighteen

Motivate Yourself: You Don't Need Steak Knives

You can motivate by fear, and you can motivate by reward. But both those methods are only temporary. The only lasting thing is self-motivation. - Homer Rice

You may just think you need a new iPad or a weekend getaway as an incentive to meet your sales goals.

But is that really what motivates you?

How about this for motivation – your nice commission check or weekly salary. That should be enough to keep most salespeople enthusiastic about their jobs.

Of course, if you need to find some additional inspiration, you should really analyze why. For example, if you have:

• Lost the passion and no longer seem to be as enthusiastic about selling, you have to evaluate the reasons why and address the problem as soon as possible. And if you can't regain your passion for sales, do something else.

• Temporary burnout, which may be the result of overwork, no vacation, and other factors, you may need to take a getaway rest or play golf this weekend instead of going into the office.

Assuming you have not lost your passion and aren't suffering from burnout, you also may face periods when you need something extra to stay on schedule. Some salespeople require more constant motivation than others.

Incentive Campaigns

You may be one of the many who have been caught up in the excitement of a company-wide incentive campaign. During a rousing speech, your sales manager announces the ambitious goals and prizes, and then you and your peers begin the competition.

I have been an incentive campaign contestant, and over the years have earned several vacation prizes, along with companywide recognition. I am now more involved in helping to create these competitions, which I believe do generate greater total company sales – even though I am not convinced they have a significant impact on the long-term success of most individual salespeople. My experience is that incentive campaigns provide short-term encouragement for people to surpass their normal quotas, but do not necessarily alter the way they perform on a routine basis. Once the contest is over, they will return to their comfort zone and resume their previous work habits.

I have also learned that most top producers aren't major fans of incentive campaigns. During the early phase of a major Gold Star sales program, I remember several of our best salespeople shaking their heads. When I asked what was bothering them, one smiled and said, "We don't need the prizes to sell more. Other than our commissions and other perks, our incentive is knowing that we are among the best."

Of course, I am not suggesting that you shouldn't participate in your company's incentive campaigns. I can imagine your sales manager's response if you should decline to join your fellow salespeople in the annual Sales Extravaganza. Ideally, you will gain some additional insights about your normal sales strategies so that you can make necessary modifications to enhance your future performance. If you refine your routine so that you sell as if you were participating in a contest every day, that contest could reward you for years to come.

Be a Spectator

The next time you participate in an incentive contest, watch what you do as if you were watching a game show, and analyze what you did to compete for the prize. Perhaps you simply worked longer hours. However, you may find that the excitement of the contest helped you come up with some really effective or innovative techniques that you could incorporate into your ongoing strategy to achieve sales superstardom.

Walking on Coals

In addition to incentive campaigns, some salespeople seek motivation by attending inspirational seminars. These programs are typically aimed at helping us overcome emotional blocks or other obstacles that prevent our optimum performance and encouraging us to take different approaches in our work and personal lives.

I have never been a huge fan of the "cheerleader"

type of motivational seminars as a sales-building strategy, although I have attended several of them. The most notable events feature a charismatic speaker directing attendees to walk over a bed of hot coals, breaking a board with one fist, or perhaps just shouting loudly in order to prompt the crowd to a standing ovation.

The problem with most such programs is that they don't keep us motivated for long. We are inspired and entertained by the speaker's message, but once we return to the office and the adrenalin wears off, we generally revert to our old habits. When I give speeches to employees or groups of salespeople, I don't lead them in push-ups or chanting exercises. I do strive to give them specific strategies they can follow once they return to their own offices. I am always hopeful that my practical suggestions do have a long-term benefit.

Long-Term Action

If you are looking for a meaningful motivational jump start that will generate permanent results, the solution may be to develop or refine your own "rewards and punishment" system. This involves providing yourself with a reward for achieving a specific goal and punishment for not meeting it. For example, if you set a goal of closing a certain number of sales by a specific time period – which could be noon, end of the day, or by end of the week – and achieve that target, you grant yourself an afternoon golf game, dinner with friends, a three-day weekend or other bonus. Conversely if you don't meet the goal, you miss out on the golf game or the steak.

Reward Yourself

Create a list of three-to-five "prizes" that you could use as incentives to achieve greater results. This could include lunch with a friend, afternoon of golf or a weekend trip. Measure your production on a daily or weekly basis, and reward or punish yourself accordingly.

To make this approach successful, you must be disciplined enough to actually take the reward, or deny yourself the bonus. In addition, you need to monitor and adjust on a frequent basis. To motivate myself, I use a combination of the rewards or punishment process, along with a laser-like focus on reaching both minor and major goals. During my sales career, I have set substantial sales targets with the promise of something special, like attending an ice hockey game or even better, a weekend trip I can share with a few of our top salespeople who have also achieved their goals. I don't recall how many times I had to deny myself the bonus, but honestly don't think it was too often.

I also have a very simple motivational approach that helps me to achieve many of my regular responsibilities. For example, I won't leave the office until I return the calls or emails that are necessary, or I will finish up from my home office.

So go ahead and compete for that iPad, or the steak knives, or that all-expenses paid trip to Las Vegas. Get rejuvenated at that "high performance" seminar. But while you're doing it, make sure your personal motivational engine is working correctly.

Chapter Nineteen
Charting Your Course: When the Going Gets Tough, Sales Superstars Thrive

Success is not final, failure is not fatal: it is the courage to continue that counts. - Winston Churchill

Okay, so now what?

I am assuming you are a hardworking, goal-oriented, proactive, "raise the bar" type of salesperson. Otherwise, you probably would not have taken the time to purchase and read this book. I hope these pages have helped you gain some valuable insights about the key strategies necessary to become a top producer in your profession, from advance planning, obtaining an assistant, and customer-for-life campaigns, to self-motivation and reinventing yourself.

Of course, you may still have a big decision to make: whether or not to continue on the challenging and exciting path to become or remain a top producer, one of the best salespeople in your field. I know that those who are truly committed will find ways to overcome any obstacles.

Others may settle for being second or third best. It's up to you.

Know Who You Are

As I have repeatedly stressed, you must never lose your passion for sales. This passion is what will help you succeed during the difficult days we all experience. I often tell our sales staff and others that if you wake up in the morning and really feel like selling, you are a born salesperson. If you get out of bed with excuses about why it will be a difficult day, or concerned that you can't reach the week's quota, you probably need to rethink your career. You can exist as an average salesperson without passion, but to reach the upper level – the focus of this book – you must have supreme enthusiasm for what you do.

While you confirm your passion, I also suggest that you consider your long-term objectives. For example, you must be certain that, deep down, you consider being a salesperson a great career. Many people start out in sales with the idea that they want to become a manager, overseeing a group of other salespeople. When I became a loan officer, my initial goal was to be a branch manager, as I believed that would be a more prestigious and financially rewarding position. Of course, I eventually realized that while sales managers have greater responsibilities, they earn less money than most good salespeople.

Success is Earned

You have already learned that you have to work hard to gain success. A friend of mine shared a story about his grandfather's arrival in America from Eastern Europe. After being processed at Ellis Island, he went to a cafeteria for lunch. He waited for someone to take his order and when no one did, a nearby woman explained, "You have to get in line, pick out what you want and pay at the other end." He later told my friend that "I soon learned that's how everything works in America. Life is a cafeteria here. You can get anything you want as long as you are willing to pay the price. You can get success, but you can't wait for someone to bring it to you. You have to get it yourself."

As I've stressed many times, failure is inevitable and usually helpful as you seek the highest levels of success. Most successful people have failed at one time or another. Henry Ford, Thomas Edison, and Abraham Lincoln all endured major business failures and other obstacles before achieving their goals. I also stumbled a few times before I could consider myself a successful salesman.

I heard another wonderful, true story that demonstrates the best traits of successful salespeople. A sales rep was traveling through the Midwest on his way to meet clients. It was a harsh winter, and as he headed to his next appointment, his car got stuck in a snowdrift. Waiting for a tow truck, he looked around the rural area and noticed a large building a short distance away.

While many salesmen would have remained in the comfort of their car until the service truck arrived, this guy bundled up and walked to the nearby facility, which turned out to be a manufacturing plant. It was a late Friday afternoon so there wasn't as much activity as usual, and he was fortunate to encounter the company's purchasing manager in the lobby. They talked about the winter weather, discovered they had mutual interests, and surprise! The salesman learned that one of his products was a staple in the company's manufacturing process.

This manufacturing plant eventually became one of the salesman's biggest customers. His passion for sales, curiosity, and determination led him to a lucrative discovery.

This salesman had developed his expertise over several years, during which he certainly had some mid-course corrections. I rarely worry about previous missteps, but occasionally consider what I could have done differently during my own sales career. These are the "what ifs" that I sometimes share in sales meetings and speeches.

One thing I would have done differently is hire an assistant earlier, which would have let me make a faster start on my goal to become a top producer. It seemed like too big a move at the time, but in hindsight this would have enabled me to focus on sales and achieve my goals a lot more rapidly.

Another step I would have taken earlier is expanding my marketing efforts. I was initially hesitant to invest my own money, but I now know this would have been a good decision.

Work With the Best

As you continue your quest to become a superstar, I also emphasize that you should associate with other goal-oriented salespeople.

Avoid slackers, the ones who aren't motivated to succeed and generally look for the easiest ways to accomplish most tasks. They're often the biggest complainers. You won't learn much about sales techniques or anything else from these underperformers. At

Gold Star, we make a special point to attract and hire only those salespeople who demonstrate enthusiasm, a positive attitude, and a commitment to excel.

Of course, you will encounter slackers within your own organization and at companies with which you do business. While you must work together at some level, try to minimize the time you associate with them. Instead, seek the company of those who can teach you something and contribute to your development as a salesperson.

I always strive to surround myself with the most talented, knowledgeable, and successful salespeople, operations managers, executives, strategic business partners, and other professionals. They have had a major influence on my overall success.

Worth the Effort

I have talked to many salespeople who asked if the benefits of being a sales superstar justify the considerable effort involved. You know my answer: of course they do! For me, the pluses of being a top producer have greatly outweighed the long hours, missed lunches, and other sacrifices. My investment in a career has balanced well with the professional and personal rewards that I have realized.

It hasn't always been an easy path, but it has been one that has taught me a great deal about perseverance, confidence, responsibility, and achieving goals. Along the way, I have also had the opportunity to help people achieve their home ownership goals. As salespeople, we are not curing diseases or making notable discoveries, but we can definitely make a difference in people's lives. We have the satisfaction of helping someone find and purchase a home, obtain an insurance policy they thought was not possible, or buy an affordable car.

My purpose in writing this book was to share some of my experiences, along with strategies and tips, that I have gained from working and talking with other knowledgeable and successful people.

Early on, I suggested that if you followed the basic recommendations, you could be on your way to achieving greater results within 90 days. That doesn't mean that you will become a superstar in three months, but rather that you are definitely headed in the right direction. If, before reading this, you were frustrated at not being able to meet your sales targets, or otherwise lacked confidence as a salesperson, I hope you now feel better equipped to succeed. And if you were already achieving sales success, you should be better prepared to reach even more ambitious goals.

Obviously, this is only part of your roadmap to becoming a top producer. My suggestion now is to forget some of the less-effective techniques you have learned in the past. Combine the proven, results-oriented strategies in this book with your own hard-earned experience, and create your ultimate guide-book for success.

In fact, I would like to hear about your successful strategies. Visit my website (www.DanMilstein.com) and share the stories of how you've used a specific technique to achieve sales success. This will be an on-going forum to showcase some of the best strategies you and other salespeople suggest.

Meanwhile, I encourage you to maintain a steady pace to reach your ultimate goals. While it may often seem like a long and sometimes frustrating journey, I am certain you will appreciate the final outcome. I wish you much success on your mission to be your very best.

Always Be Closing.

About the Author

Daniel Milstein is known as a successful business executive, author, job creator, company builder, entrepreneur, and founder and CEO of Gold Star Mortgage Financial Group, an *Inc.* 500 Company.

Born in Kiev, Ukraine, Dan and his family experienced hardship, religious persecution, and life-and-death situations, all in the shadows of one of the greatest disasters that ever occurred, the explosion at the Chernobyl nuclear plant. Forced to escape the Soviet government, Dan's family fled to Ann Arbor, Michigan. Highly motivated to succeed, Dan worked his way up from mopping floors in a McDonald's restaurant, through a series of difficult and challenging jobs, to ultimately establish one of the 15 fastest-growing financial services companies in the United States.

He graduated with honors from Cleary University, earning a business degree, and was awarded an honorary doctorate from his alma mater. He is currently in his second term on the Cleary University Board of Trustees.

Under Dan's leadership, Gold Star has grown to be a national leader in the mortgage industry, with offices across the U.S. The company has been named a Top Workplace in Michigan by the *Detroit Free Press*, and a Michigan Economic Bright Spot by *Corp!* magazine.

Dan has been ranked the #1 loan officer in the United States, out of more than 550,000 professionals in the lending industry. He has been included in the prestigious "40 Under 40" in *Crain's* magazine, "30 in Their Thirties" in *DBusiness* magazine, and has been named one of the nation's 40 Top Finance Professionals by *National Mortgage Professional* magazine.

Dan is the author of *The ABC of Sales: Lessons from a Superstar*, and *17 Cents & a Dream: My Incredible Journey from the USSR to Living the American Dream*. He is also a contributing writer for multiple business publications. As an author, he has earned numerous awards and honors at national and international book festivals in Paris, New York, Los Angeles, San Francisco, and New England.

In 2012, Milstein was named to the prestigious National Academy of Best-Selling Authors.

Acknowledgments

Writing this book has been an incredibly positive experience, but it's clear that producing a work like this is not a one-person job. A book may be the author's vision and words, but many other people play a vital role along the way.

As I did in *The ABC of Sales*, I have numerous people to acknowledge. Some of them at Gold Star and elsewhere offered more general support, while others were more directly involved in the creation of this book.

I want to thank the management team and everyone else at Gold Star who have worked so hard during the last several years to make our company a success. Special thanks to the salespeople who took their time to offer tips and other ideas on various subjects in the book.

I am extremely appreciative of the significant commitment by Matt Roslin, a Gold Star board member and Chair of our Audit Committee. He has provided expert counsel and a unique service that have given me great peace of mind.

I certainly applaud those who were instrumental in the book's actual development and production. I am especially grateful to David Robinson who contributed his editorial skills and creativity, as he also did for *The ABC of Sales*. We have enjoyed a special, collaborative association.

Thanks to my good friend, singer, Billboard Top 10 songwriter, and producer Mike Posner for writing the Foreword. I will always cherish the good times and laughs we shared during the Winter Olympics in Sochi, Russia.

I also thank Mike Ball for his invaluable editorial assistance. We again benefitted from Scott Lorenz's expertise in the publishing and promotion phases of *Street Smart Selling*. In addition, Marty Bucella's illustrations are a special addition to this book.

I am fortunate to have been able to work with such a professional team.

I would also like to acknowledge several people who offered their insights about various aspects of the sales profession: Terri Murphy; Paul Bishop; James Nellis; Doug Smith; Bryan Ashe; Phil Harriman; Tony Franchi; Jim Hennessy; Eric Thelen; Melinda

Estridge; Michael Hellickson; Robert Ten Eyck; Erich Pergler; Ron Schwartz; the faculty, College of Management and MBA students of Cleary University; Jim Applegate; Joey DeMilio; Bill Sizer; Tom Fleming; Tim Krukowski; Lon Safko; Gary Rogers; Fred Noce; Daniel Harkavy; Dr. David Mielke and Dr. Kerry Johnson.

Lastly, I thank all of the new and veteran salespeople who have shared their own sales stories. Your desire to succeed helped motivate me to write this book, which I hope gives you additional incentive to be one of the best. ABC! (Always Be Closing)…

Dan Milstein

Index

17 Cents & a Dream 175

A

advertising 25, 32, 121, 122, 125, 127
agenda 141
Always Be Closing i, 19, 172, 178
Amy Jo Martin 130
assistant 24, 38, 67, 68, 69, 70, 71, 72, 73, 74, 75, 76, 119, 165, 169

B

Bezos, Jeff 77
budget 24, 62, 120, 122, 124, 128, 129, 144, 148
burnout 71, 159
business groups 19, 46

C

Churchill, Winston 165
Cleary University 84, 89, 174, 175, 178
closing ratio 57, 58
Coaches 144, 145
coaching 144, 147, 150
compensation 16
competition 6, 23, 27, 37, 41, 46, 47, 141, 156, 157, 160
Corp! magazine 175
Crain's magazine 175

D

decision makers 63
demographic 133, 141, 153

M

Mandino, Og 1
market vii, 18, 19, 23, 30, 31, 32, 39, 43, 46, 49, 97, 119, 122, 123, 129, 136, 143, 154, 156
market conditions 18, 31
marketing 8, 15, 23, 24, 25, 27, 35, 46, 55, 56, 68, 69, 72, 93, 94, 108, 119, 120, 121, 122, 123, 124, 125, 126, 127, 128, 129, 132, 133, 136, 141, 142, 147, 169
marketplace 23, 26, 86
mentor 2, 148
Michigan Economic Bright Spot 175
Misner, Ivan 101
motivation vi, vii, 3, 12, 15, 16, 17, 20, 87, 158, 159, 161, 165

N

National Academy of Best-Selling Authors 175
National Mortgage Professional magazine 175
networking 103
niche 42, 104

O

objections v, 59, 60, 63, 73, 85, 86
online education 144
online tracking 32, 99, 104, 127, 131, 141, 144

P

passion 38, 81, 124, 159, 160
perks 15, 160
planning 21, **22**, 25, 26, 27, 31, 32, 35, 64, 84, 85, 154, 156, 165

Made in the USA
Middletown, DE
07 November 2019

78123154R00113